How to Make a Clipper Ship Model

E. Armitage McCann

DOVER PUBLICATIONS, INC.
New York

Published in Canada by General Publishing Company, Ltd., 30 Lesmill Road, Don Mills, Toronto, Ontario.

Bibliographical Note

This Dover edition, first published in 1995, is an unabridged republication of the work originally published by the Norman W. Henley Publishing Company, New York, in 1926, under the title *Ship Model Making, Volume II: How to Make a Model of the American Clipper Ship Sovereign of the Seas Simplified or With Complete Details*. The original color frontispiece has been reprinted in black and white for this edition, on page viii; some other illustrations have also been repositioned.

Library of Congress Cataloging-in-Publication Data

McCann, E. Armitage.
   [Ship model making. Volume 2]
   How to make a clipper ship model / E. Armitage McCann.
      p.   cm.
   Originally published: Ship model making, v. 2: How to make a model of the American clipper ship. New York : Norman W. Henley Pub. Co., 1926.
   Includes index.
   ISBN 0-486-28580-4 (pbk.)
   1. Ship models.   2. Clipper ships—Models.   I. Title.
VM298.M394   1995
623.8'20124—dc20   94–46480
                                                              CIP

Manufactured in the United States of America
Dover Publications, Inc., 31 East 2nd Street, Mineola, N.Y. 11501

PREFACE

THERE is a large and apparently increasing number of people—men and women, boys and girls—who hanker to make ship models of their own. This, to me, is not surprising. I like to have them and I like to make them myself. The kind I like best of all are the clippers; partly because they are the type of vessel I sailed on in my younger days and partly because, in their lines, they have a beauty all their own. I find many others with discerning eyes who also appreciate this attribute.

Some people there are who prefer the galleon and caraval type of ship. Certainly, they are more decorative with their gaily-colored sails, hulls and carved and gilded poops and forecastles. To these persons the first volume of this series appeals.

I wish to state here that in speaking of ship models I am not alluding to what may be termed "store models." These are not at all like any ship that ever floated so they are not really models at all, but are decorations with a ship motif. As such they have their place, but it is not in the homes of people genuinely interested in real ships.

The galleons, no matter how beautiful, have not the austere beauty of the clippers—a workmanlike beauty that has been evolved through designing for carrying with speed which entails the knowledge of how to make use of and, if necessary, combat the natural forces of wind and sea.

I long hesitated before endeavoring to describe how to make a model of a clipper ship, for familiarity with the sailing of clippers and making models of them made me realize the intricacy of them—both in hull and rigging—and I preferred to see none made rather than poor ones.

However, in view of the immediate and unexpected success of my Spanish Galleon and Pirate Ship Instructions, the editor of Popular Science Magazine persuaded me to write instructions on similar lines for making a clipper. So, for that magazine, I described how to make a simplified model of the clipper "Sovereign of the Seas." To this editor I am indebted for permission to use the material then published, which here can find a permanent home with more space in which to describe all the details of the building and rigging processes.

I have here endeavoured to take the building and rigging, step by step, from the raw material to the finished model, with ample descriptions and illustrations, so that the novice with no exact knowledge of ships can make a really worth while model. To this I have added detailed data which will enable the experienced craftsman to bring his ship to an exact and perfect finish.

There are those abroad in the land who just have to make a ship model whether they have information on the subject or not—the urge is there and must be satisfied. Their results may be fair, more often poor or even bad, but they cannot be good unless they work to scale plans. There are some plans readily obtainable but they have to be interpreted into terms of wood, cord, etc., and this requires a special knowledge.

It is for these people especially, I have written this book, though the expert has by no means been forgotten. From the short description given in the magazine really fine models have been made, therefore I am convinced that from this book they can be made, even more easily and perfectly.

PREFACE

I purposely made the original without any special tools, material or elaborate workshop, in order that anyone can follow me. I had great enjoyment in making it and think that you will find intense pleasure in the work itself and be proud and happy in the result—a scale model of the *"Sovereign of the Seas."*

E. Armitage McCann.

November, 1931.

MAIN-YARD BACKED

CLIPPER SHIP
SOVEREIGN
OF THE
SEAS

CONTENTS

86 working drawings accompanying text.

Working plans for the larger parts of the ship, in pocket on the inside of back cover.

Engraving of "The Sovereign of the Seas" from the Illustrated London News of May, 1859.

"This celebrated American clipper ship arrived in the Mersey on the 2nd inst. having made the run in a shorter time than was previously accomplished by a sailing ship."

INTRODUCTION

IN THIS BOOK will be found complete instructions for building a model of America's most beautiful Clipper Ship the *"Sovereign of the Seas,"* either simplified or with complete detail.

By "simplified" is meant that as much detail as possible that is difficult to make is omitted, provided such elimination does not materially injure the aspect of the model as a whole. This method tends to make the work much less arduous. For any but the very skilled workman, it is to be recommended in building a small scale model, because unless the parts omitted are very well made, to scale, they give the model a clumsy appearance. This, above all things, is to be avoided, and to the writer's thinking is more injurious than their omission.

The scale of $\frac{1}{12}$ inch to the foot of the real ship has been chosen because that makes a model of suitable size for the average room, and because with this scale it is possible, with the book and plans to be found in the envelope on the back cover, to present everything required of the actual size they are to be made, thus saving enlarging, with its consequent liability to error.

The simplified model will, if made as described, be true to scale, just as though it has been made with greater elaboration.

There are, however, those who wish their model to be a careful reproduction of the real ship to the last rope-yarn; who have the skill and do not object to the time expended, provided the result is the best it is possible to attain. Bearing these in mind, as additions to the various instructions, minutely exact details are given of each part of any importance, with suggestions for making them.

It is suggested that those desiring to make this latter type of model, should do so to a larger scale than that given, for which purpose information is given in the first chapter.

Lest this may read as though trying to discourage fellow workers from attempting the complete scale model, I wish emphatically to say that such is not my object; the more that make the complete model the better I will be pleased, and having got so far as the making of the simple model requires, it seems a pity not to "go the whole hog"; all I insist upon, is that a good simple model is better than a bad elaborate one, of which there are far more to be seen than there should be.

The reasons for the methods adopted of building the hull and other parts are given in the third chapter.

The making of this model will need a good deal of work, requiring some handiness with tools and nimble fingers, but does not entail any very great difficulties, and though the work may appear complicated at a glance, yet, if it is taken step by step, as described, it will be found that it will all work out quite easily to a triumphant finish, with the hoisting of the Stars and Stripes.

An advantage in ship-model building over other crafts is that most things are not good to look at until complete or nearly so, and consequently have to be kept out of sight until finished, but the ship model is beautiful and interesting almost from the very commencement. For those who can only spare a little time for the work this is a distinct advantage, because they have something worth looking at right along, which grows in interest as parts are added.

INTRODUCTION

The *"Sovereign of the Seas"* was chosen for description for several reasons. She was, in the opinion of many, the finest of Donald McKay's famous clipper ships, as far as beauty of line is concerned, and that is saying a great deal.

Donald McKay may confidently be named as America's most famous shipbuilder of the time when American ships lead the whole world in speed and beauty. His ships have never been surpassed in either of these qualities. They were white winged things of beauty that through storm and calm, manned by skillful, daring men, carried America's flag and commerce to the far ends of the earth, and earned many of the early fortunes upon which the prosperity of this country is established.

Yankee clippers did more than this. They fought their rivals on their own ground and, for a time, through sheer merit, snatched cargoes from their rival's foreign strongholds and carried them right to their very own doors.

This *"Sovereign of the Seas"* must not, through similarity of name, be confused with the line-of-battle ship of 1637, nor with a medium clipper built in 1868.

Of her, Arthur H. Clark, in his "Clipper Ship Era," published by G. P. Putnam's Sons, says:

"Undismayed by difficulties as to spars and rigging that beset the minds of other ship-builders, Donald McKay resolved in this year to build a still larger clipper than had yet appeared. This ship was the *Sovereign of the Seas,* of 2421 tons register, and when she was launched in June, 1852, the bells that had welcomed the *New World* and *Stag-Hound* as the largest merchant ships afloat, again rang out a joyous greeting to this noble clipper, as she glided smoothly and swiftly into the blue waters of Boston harbor.

The *Sovereign of the Seas* measured; length 258 feet,

breadth 44 feet, depth 23 feet 6 inches, with 20 inches dead-rise at half floor. It is interesting to note that each one of Mr. McKay's clippers had less dead-rise than her predecessor. The *Stag-Hound* had 40 inches dead-rise at half floor with slightly convex water-lines; the *Flying Cloud* and *Staffordshire* 30 inches with concave water-lines and shorter but sharper ends. The *Sovereign of the Seas* had the longest and sharpest ends of any vessel then built, and combined the grace and beauty of the smaller ships with immense strength and power to carry sail.

She had a crew of 105 men and boys, consisting of 4 mates, 2 boatswains, 2 carpenters, 2 sailmakers, 3 stewards, 2 cooks, 80 able seamen, and 10 boys before the mast. She was commanded by Captain Lauchlan Mc-Kay, who was born at Shelburne, Nova Scotia, in 1811, being one year younger than his brother Donald. Like him, he went to New York, served an apprenticeship there with Isaac Webb, and after becoming a master shipwright, was appointed carpenter of the U. S. frigate *Constellation,* in which he served four years. Admiral Farragut was a young lieutenant on board this ship at the same time. In 1839 Captain McKay published a work on naval architecture, and soon after, in company with his brother Hugh, opened a shipyard at Boston. Here they did repairing, and in 1846 built the bark *Odd Fellow,* in which Lauchlan sailed as captain. In 1848 he commanded the ship *Jenny Lind,* and made some excellent passages in her. When he took command of the *Sovereign of the Seas,* Captain McKay was in his forty-first year, and of gigantic build and strength.

The *Sovereign of the Seas* sailed from New York for San Francisco, August 4, 1852, a poor season of the year for a rapid run to the equator, but she crossed 25 days out from Sandy Hook, making a run which had never been bettered in the month of August, and only twice equalled—once by the *Raven* from Boston in 1851 and once by the *Hurricane* from New York in 1853. She was 23 days from the equator to 50° S., and 9 days from 50° S. in the Atlantic to the same parallel in the Pacific. After rounding Cape Horn, she carried away her fore and maintopmasts and foreyard, and it required fourteen days to rerig her, during which time she was kept on her course, and made the run from 50° S. to the equator in the remarkable time, considering her disabled condition, of 29 days. She went thence to San Francisco in 17 days, which is the record for the month of November, and her total run from New York to San Francisco was 103 days.

Had the *Sovereign of the Seas* not been dismasted, it is reasonable to suppose that she would have equalled the fastest run from 50° S. to the equator in the month of October, which is 19 days, made by the *Ocean Telegraph* in 1855. This would have reduced her passage to 93 days; still, as it stands, her passage of 103 days has never been equalled by a vessel sailing from New York for San Francisco in the month of August. Captain McKay received much credit for rerigging his ship at sea and not putting into Valparaiso, and was presented with a very beautiful silver dinner service by the New York Board of Marine Underwriters.

This was the only passage made by the *Sovereign of the Seas* between New York, and San Francisco. She carried on this voyage 2950 tons of cargo, and her freight amounted to $84,000; a portion of the cargo, consisting of flour, sold in San Francisco at $44 per barrel.

She cleared from San Francisco in ballast for Honolulu, and there loaded a cargo, or rather several cargoes, of sperm oil which had been landed by American whale-ships in the Pacific, and sailed for New York, February 13, 1853. She had light and variable winds to the equator, her day's runs ranging from 89 to 302 miles, and she made this stretch from Honolulu in 8 days. On February 27th, she was off the Navigator or Samoan Islands, and one cannot help thinking of the delight it would have given Robert Louis Stevenson if he could have looked upon this giant clipper flying southward under her white cloud of canvas, and with what magic words he would have made her name immortal.

On March 4th, the *Sovereign of the Seas* sprung her foretopmast, and although it was fished on the 6th, it was a source of anxiety for the remainder of the passage, and Captain McKay, mindful of his recent experience in these seas, carried sail with a considerable caution. Nothing of special interest occurred until March 15th, when the first strong westerly gales were felt, and a series of remarkable day's runs was begun. Up to noon on March 16th, she had sailed from her position at noon the day before, 396 miles; on the 17th, 311 miles; on the 18th, 411 miles, and on the 19th, 360 miles, a total of 1478 miles in four days. During these four days, she made 34° 43' of longitude eastward, which with the difference in time gives an average of 15½ knots, or an average of a fraction over 378 miles for each twenty-four hours. In the 11 days from March 10th to the 21st, she made the remarkable run of 3562 miles, and as she made during this time 82° 24' of longitude, her average allowing for difference in time, was 13¾ knots, or 330 miles each twenty-four hours.

During her great run on the 18th of 411 miles, she made 10° 30' of longitude, which reduced her sea day to 23 hours 18 minutes, and shows an average speed of

17⅔ knots, or 424 miles in twenty-four hours. On this day her log records: "Strong northwest breezes and rough sea." It seems extremely improbable that she could have maintained uniform speed of 17⅔ knots throughout the twenty-four hours, but at times her speed probably slackened to 15 or 16 knots. If this supposition is correct, it follows that her speed must at times have exceeded 17⅔ knots in order to account for this average. In the absence of any data on this point, which is much to be regretted, it seems probable that she must have sailed at a speed of not less than 19 knots during a portion of these twenty-four hours, and perhaps 20 knots. After rounding Cape Horn she had light and moderate winds, her best day's run being only 286 miles, and she arrived off Sandy Hook May 6, 1853, after a passage of 82 days from Honolulu.

She sailed again from New York for Liverpool, June 18th, passing Sandy Hook at 6:30 P. M., sighted Cape Race in Newfoundland at 6 A. M., on the 24th, was off Cape Clear in Ireland at 6 A. M. on June 30th, took a pilot at 2 P. M., July 2nd, and anchored in the Mersey at 10:30 P. M. that day, having made the entire run from dock to anchorage in 13 days 22 hours and 50 minutes. This must be regarded as a most remarkable passage for the season, and has never been equalled by a sailing vessel during the month of June. Her best day's run was on June 28th, 344 miles, by the wind, under single-reefed topsails, and on the 30th, 340 miles with skysails and royal studding-sails set. The Cunard S. S. *Canada* sailed from Boston on the same day that the *Sovereign of the Seas* sailed from New York, and a comparison of their logs published at the time shows that in five days, June 25-30th, the ship outsailed the steamer by 325 miles, and that the best run of the *Canada* during this passage was only 306 miles.

On this voyage her builder, Donald McKay, was a passenger on board the *Sovereign of the Seas,* and he passed most of his waking moments on deck, watching her movement through the water and observing the various strains on her spars and rigging. When he returned home, Enoch Train asked him what he thought of the ship, and Mr. McKay replied, "Well, she appears to be a pretty good ship, but I think I can build one to beat her"; and eventually he did so.

Mrs. Donald McKay sailed with her husband on this voyage and took a keen interest in everything that went on aboard ship. Although this was a summer passage, nevertheless, there was enough rough weather to bring out the splendid sea-going qualities of the vessel, and to Mrs. McKay, who, it is a pleasure to record, is still living, the vivid picture of this thoroughbred clipper wrestling with the winds and waves has always remained one of the exciting experiences of her life.

She was originally owned by Grinnell, Minturn Co. of New York.

The *Sovereign of the Seas* had attracted much attention upon her arrival at Liverpool in 1853, and was almost immediately chartered to load for Australia in the Black Ball Line. It is to be regretted that for some reason Captain McKay gave up charge of the ship and returned to the United States, the command being given to Captain Warner, who had no previous experience in handling American clipper ships, although he proved an extremely competent commander. The *Sovereign of the Seas* sailed from Liverpool September 7, 1853, and arrived at Melbourne after a passage of 77 days. In a letter from Melbourne Captain Warner gives the following account of this passage:

"I arrived here after a long and tedious passage of 77 days, having experienced only light and contrary winds the greater part of the passage—I have had but two chances. The ship ran in four consecutive days 1275 miles; and the next run was 3375 miles in twelve days. These were but moderate chances. I was 31 days to the Equator and carried skysails 65 days; set them on leaving Liverpool, and never shortened them for 35 days. Crossed the Equator in 26° 30′, and went to 53° 30′ south, but found no strong winds. Think if I had gone to 58° south, I would have had wind enough; but the crew were insufficiently clothed, and about one half disabled, together with the first mate. At any rate, we have beaten all and every one of the ships that sailed with us, and also the famous English clipper *Gauntlet* ten days on the passage, although the *Sovereign of the Seas* was loaded down to twenty-three and one half feet." On the homeward voyage she brought the mails and over four tons of gold-dust, and made the passage in 68 days. On this voyage there was a mutiny among the crew, who intended to seize the ship and capture the treasure. Captain Warner acted with great firmness and tact in supressing the mutineers and placing them in irons without loss of life, for which he received much credit.

The *Sovereign of the Seas* was sold to a Hamburg firm and was wrecked on the Pyramid Shoal in the Straits of Malacca, August 6, 1859, becoming a total loss.

This then is a brief account of some of her more noteworthy achievements. An early government publication credits her with a day's run of 436 miles, which equals the world's record made by the *"Flying Cloud."* I believe this is an error, but she does not need it added to her laurels as she has plenty without. There are only about twenty super-steamships at present afloat which could beat her when she had the wind. The trouble which led to the almost complete extinction of sailing vessels, was that they did not always have the wind, and therefore were more uncertain than steamships in the length of their passages, and also that they had to carry a large crew, which did not matter so much when their wages were so trifling, but is an important factor now.

It is now up to you to make a model worthy of such a wonderful ship—a model that will convince you and your friends that a clipper ship was the most beautiful thing ever wrought by the hands of man. Go to it!

THE FINISH

ADDITIONAL NOTES

Hull Line Plan

Forecastle: Cut the after end, as shown on Deck Plan, $\frac{1}{2}$ in. abaft line III. Cut the fore end, as shown on the Breadth Plan, to $3\frac{3}{4}$ in. before line III.

Poop: Cut to the lines shown on Breadth Plan and glue on with forward edge to the position shown on Deck Plan, thus giving a slightly longer counter (stern Profile) curve.

Bulwarks: Carry the rabbet about $\frac{1}{2}$ in. further aft than shown on Sheer Plan, making the bulwark pieces that much longer and thus giving better nailage.

Ends of lifts: These appear slightly confused on the Breadth Plan. Cut them to the lengths shown on Sheer Plan but leave a bit long and shape to Sheer Plan lines when glued up.

Sail Plan

The rake of the masts are correctly given on page 99, but on the Sail Plan the foremast rakes $\frac{3}{16}$ in. too much, measured from the deck to the cap.

The position of the bumkins is correctly given here, and not as on the Sheer Plan. They should be $\frac{1}{8}$ in. forward of line XIII.

The stays are, I believe, correct for this ship but would look better in the usual position for ships of this period, which would be: Mizzen-skysail-stay to main-topmast cap; main-skysail-stay to fore-topgallantmast-head; main-royal-stay to fore-topmast-cap; the others as shown.

Page xiii. The length of the Sovereign of the Seas is given in some accounts as 258 feet. Her lines only give 248 feet. She may have been built longer than originally planned. The 248 feet length has been adhered to, but if the longer length is desired add $\frac{1}{2}$ in. on either side of line viii.

There is also a difference of 4 ft. between her lines and description, as our lines give 40 feet beam. This can be added if desired.

It is suggested, however, that it would be wise to keep to her original authenticated lines, as here given.

Page 21. Cord: The rigging of the real ship varied from 12 in. diameter for the lower shrouds to 1 in. for the royal braces.

All the standing rigging is black and the running rigging, brown (tarred hemp) or manilla color. None of it it white.

Blocks are white or brown.

Page 43. *Figurehead.* Some descriptions of this give her a figurehead representing a sea god, half man, half fish with a conch shell raised in the act of blowing; painted bronze. There is no picture of this.

Page 44. *Waterways.* Further explanation: Lay and glue the waterways ($\frac{1}{8}$ x $\frac{1}{16}$ in.) in the corner formed by the deck and bulwarks. Then glue the stanchions (timberheads) to these and the bulwarks. If some of the timberheads are pointed and glued into holes through the waterways into the hull, it will make a firmer job.

Page 89. The trucks were gilded.

Page 99. *Ratlines.* No. 60 cotton would be better. The ratlines on model B, should be clove-hitched to each shroud.

Page 113. The skysail, royal, and topgallant braces

will be of the thinnest cord.   Topsail braces and pendants of the lower braces (when not chain) will be medium cord and purchases of the lower braces of the thin cord.

Page 116.   Above the cheeks, the lowermast-head was probably square.

Page 124.   Deadeyes and lanyards are always black.

Page 125.   The space between the deadeyes of the lower shrouds is 2 to $2\frac{1}{2}$ times the diameter of the dead-eyes.   The drift between the topmast-backstay deadeyes is about one diameter more.

Page 128.   Fig. LXXIV.   The holes in the lower row of deadeyes are incorrectly placed.

Page 133.   *Topsail braces.*   The standing parts of the whips of these at the main should be fastened to bolts at the fore end of the mizzen channels, the hauling parts leading to the rail as shown on the sail plan.

Page 144.   *Side Lights.*   These were optional until 1858, but were usually carried; frequently in the fore-rigging.

E. A. M.

November, 1931.

MODEL OF "THE SOVEREIGN OF THE SEAS."—Made by the Author.

SHIP MODEL MAKING

VOL. II

CHAPTER I

HINTS AND DEFINITIONS

SCALE as referred to in this book has nothing to do with fishes; scale here means the relative proportion of the linear dimensions of the parts of the model, to the dimensions of the corresponding parts of the ship represented, and this working to scale, it must be insisted, is most vital in making every part of the ship. If working to the scale of $\frac{1}{12}$ inch to the foot, see to it that, as near as possible, every foot of the real ship is represented by $\frac{1}{12}$ of an inch in the model, or if working to any other scale that the parts are enlarged accurately so as to preserve the scale being worked to, throughout.

If working to any other scale than that given of $\frac{1}{12}$ in. = 1 ft. full sized drawings of every part should be made before proceeding.

Though smaller models than that given, can be made, it is only the very skilled that in them can preserve the scale, especially in the spars and rigging, and when finished they are inclined to be either clumsy or fragile.

The size given makes a hull of $19\frac{1}{4}$ in. on the waterline and an over all length of 26 in. by $16\frac{1}{2}$ height, which is a good size for the average small room, and sufficiently strong to withstand the onslaughts of the feather duster.

For a model of this size, the writer would prefer the simplified (or sketch) model, (which will be referred to throughout the book as Model A.) with perhaps some of the deck furnishings more carefully made, that is, unless the maker is an exceptionally clever workman with just the right fine tools. His reason for this is that it is possible for the amateur to thus keep his model more slender and graceful looking, than if he fussed it up with many small parts, which are fine to examine closely but not necessary for the general appearance.

If, on the other hand, the reader decides that he wants the best and nothing but—that he wants a really exact replica of the ship, with every last detail aloft and alow, then the additional notes given will serve his purpose as thoroughly as the writer can devise, in the limited space of one book.

Such a model should, however, be made to a larger scale, to be not less than $\frac{1}{8}$ inch to the foot, or for preference $\frac{1}{6}$th. To make it $\frac{1}{8}$th, every part (except those given on that scale) should be enlarged by one-half; for a $\frac{1}{6}$th inch scale the parts should be doubled, and so forth.

The extra details will be described as for Model B.

It may be commented that the writer says "keep the scale" and then does not do it. The answer is that on so small a model it is not always wise; thus for example, the skysail yards should have 6 in. diameter tapering to 3 in. at the yard arms, which to $\frac{1}{12}$ in. scale would make them $\frac{1}{48}$ in. diameter at those points and that is quite small. The braces for this yard would be not more than one inch equalling 144th inch, or as the finest sewing silk and unsuitable for anything but a glass-case model, and the upper parts thus having to be over scale the corre-

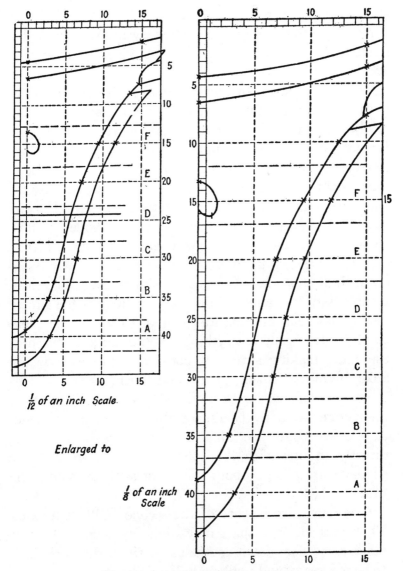

$\frac{1}{12}$ of an inch Scale.

Enlarged to

$\frac{1}{8}$ of an inch
Scale

FIG. I.—Method of enlarging drawings.

[3]

sponding parts below have been made slightly over scale also, to preserve the proportion.

As this overscaling is not necessary in a larger model the actual size of the smaller parts is given on the plans and illustrations.

The two most important things to remember are that most models are spoiled by having a misshapen hull and too heavy spars. The sailor is particularly prone to the former fault, because he builds by eye and probably has never seen the under-water body of his ship. If making the model at sea, he most likely has to do this, because no plans are available, and he would not know how to read them if he had them, but when he makes models ashore he should use lines, like everyone else who wants a true hull, because even the most accurate eyes are not reliable on such fine work. The reader should have but little trouble with this angle of the work, if he uses the simple method laid out, but, naturally, great care must be exer-cised in truing-up everything to the lines given and especially making sure that both sides are everywhere alike, by measurement, by eye and touch.

Some people can even a curved part best by running their fingers over it, others by sight. To see if both sides of a curved part are alike, hold it up to the eye level, directly in line with the source of light, so that the shadows are alike on both sides, but apply measurement first and last.

One must also beware of the second fault mentioned. Though the lighter spars may advisedly be a shade over-scale, keep them down as fine as possible; they are likely to be too heavy and unlikely to be too light.

Another point to be careful about, throughout, is that everything is truly central, or "on the line of the keel." The keel (see large plan and Fig. XIV) is the ship's backbone, and the position and line of *all* parts are related to it. The stem and stern must be vertical to it on the same line; the deck is at a right angle to it, with equal breadth on either side of its line; the bowsprit extends forward along the same line; the masts start centrally over it and extend upwards truly vertical to it, which is the same line as the stem and sternpost; but they rake aft at an angle sligtly less than a right angle with it; the center of the yards are hung to the masts (right over it) and are at a right angle to it, in line with the deck; all the deck fittings are centrally over it or at equi-distances from it. The water-line is the line of measurement, but the keel is the "base" for all angular measurement.

The largest of the parts are but small, thus it is recommended that they do not be sawed too close to the lines, but that a little be left for sandpapering, especially with the softwood, which rubs down so quickly, a final flat surface is best arrived at by laying the sandpaper on a flat surface and rubbing the piece on that, holding it firmly and rubbing evenly.

For very fine work it should be remembered that a coat or two of paint or varnish add appreciably to the thickness.

Regarding the painting as a whole, it should be remembered that one is not making a sleek yacht nor a coal hulk, nor even a genuine antique galleon—price $7.50.

These clippers were very smart and well kept up, but they received a great deal of battering by the weather and by lying alongside all sorts of quays; therefore though nothing should be dishevelled, rough or actually discolored, neither should the model be shiny or too new looking.

The finer ships usually had elaborately ornamented cabins, panelled in four or five different fine woods—

bird's eye maple mirrors and red plush being the acme of ship interior decoration of those days; outside the decoration was restrained and consisted of finely carved mahogany or teak brackets, and posts, with door and window moldings and the like. The figureheads and scrollwork were splendid carvings, and many ships had additional carving round the stern; some ships had the figureheads in realistic colors, but beyond that there would be no color, anywhere, except in the sidelights, when shipped, and the flags.

Nevertheless, though the ship is black and white, it can be colorful; the underwater body will be bronze or green copper color, the black sides have color in them— black is seldom black; and the masts and cordage have color. Do not be tempted, to add scarlet, blue and yellow to taste, nor to leave nice gilt chains that way, nor to have little figures running round the deck or aloft— they turn your scale model into a child's toy, and not a good one at that.

The order in which the work is described need not be adhered to in doing it; for example: one can be making the deck fittings while the several coats of paint are drying on the hull, or when one feels like doing some fine work sitting down; the spars should all be made some days before they are required, so that the paint and varnish on them will be thoroughly dry and so forth.

Knots

Just a few knots, hitches and seizings will be needed, and should be practised before the work of rigging is begun.

There are many books which give a full range of knots and splices, but to save the uninitiated the trouble of get-

HINTS AND DEFINITIONS

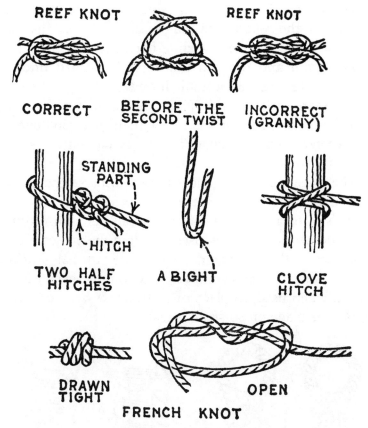

FIG. II.—Requisite knots.

ting one of these the few required will be described and
may be seen in Fig. II.

The reef (or square) knot, shown first, is for tying
the ends of cords together. If made right it is the most
handy all-round knot in existance, if made wrong it is
a danger, and the only way to invariably get it right is
to watch the second twist, note that after the first twist
the ends keep to their own side before making the second
twist—the end that comes up away from you stops away
and the end next to you stops there until again twisted.

The next cut is of two-half-hitches, made by taking the end of the rope round the object it is to be fastened to, then round its own standing part, through the bight, round again and through the bight. A third hitch is never wanted, in fact any hitch on top of a good one is worse than useless. One good knot is better than any number of bad ones and is better than two good ones—the second is entirely superfluous. A half-hitch is one-half of two-half-hitches.

The clove hitch is frequently used to make the end or middle of a rope fast to something fixed, especially when there is to be a strain in both directions, as with ratlines. In model work it is often used to retain the end of a cord more neatly than can be done with the two-half-hitches.

The next knot shown is required for the ends of lanyards, when used, in place of a Matthew Walker which cannot be made on so small a scale.

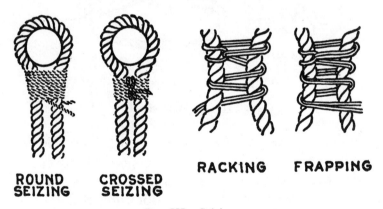

ROUND SEIZING   CROSSED SEIZING   RACKING   FRAPPING

Fig. III.—Seizings.

Seizings

Seizings, rackings and frappings, are, for our work, very similar and consist of the binding of two heavy cords with a thinner one. (See Fig. III.)

A seizing is the joining of two ropes, or the two ends

of one rope together, by taking several turns of small rope or line round them. End seizing is a round seizing on the end of a rope. Throat seizing is the first seizing clapped on where a rope or ropes cross each other. Middle seizing is a seizing between a throat and an end seizing. Eye seizing is a round seizing next the eye of a shroud or other object.

A cross seizing, is a seizing with a few turns taken round its other parts, to further tighten them.

A frapping is taking several turns round the middle of a lashing or of other ropes, drawing the several parts together.

A racking is very similar but with the turns passed differently, and more often of a temporary nature.

A lashing is a rope which by one or more turns fastens any one thing to another, such as: two ropes, a rope to a spar, a spar to a ring-bolt, etc.

If you can make splices small enough for this work you will need no assistance from me.

Definitions

It is quite impossible to talk about ships, to say nothing of making one, without using some technical words, because they are the only ones that describe the part or action.

Every name used for a part of this ship will be described in words or illustration as the work proceeds and such other words as are used in proceeding, fairly well describe themselves. Nearly every modern book one picks up has a glossary, and any good dictionary explains the words, however, that there may be no confusion, such sea terms as are here used will be briefly defined.

Abaft or Aft. The hinder part of a ship, or all those

parts which lie towards the stern. Frequently used to signify further aft, or nearer the stern.

Aboard or Inboard. Inside, or on the ship.

Abreast. Side by side or opposite to.

A-head. Movement towards the head of the ship. Also used in opposition to A-stern, the former implies at any distance before the ship, the latter behind.

Alongside. At the side of the ship, outside it.

Aloft. Anywhere in the rigging or on the mast fittings.

Amidships or 'Midships. The middle of the ship, with regard to her length or breadth.

A-stern. The opposite to ahead, which see.

Athwart—Athwartships. Across. (A Thwart is a boat's seat).

Belaying. Fastening a rope by giving it several cross turns alternately round two timberheads, cleats or a belaying pin.

Bends. The small rope used to lash the clinch of a cable, also some of the knots fastening two rope-ends together.

To bend. To bring something into use by putting it in position. Thus one may "bend" a sail by fastening it to the yard, or bend a hat by wearing it for the first time.

Bight. The double part of a rope when it is folded. (See Fig. II).

Bousing. Bowsing. Hauling or pulling upon a rope or fall of a tackle to remove a body, or increase the tension.

Bow. The front end of a ship.

Bright-work. Wood that is scrubbed bare or varnished. The opposite to paint-work.

Capsize. To upset or turn over.

Carry away. To break.

Chocks. Cut out blocks of wood, for boats, spars, etc., to rest in, as cradles. A wedge retaining anything.

Chock-a-block. The same as block-and-block. The situation of a tackle when the effect is destroyed, by the blocks meeting together.

Clap on. To fasten or lay hold of. Also used to the act of setting more sail.

Cleats. Pieces of wood of various shapes, used for stops, and to make ropes fast to.

Coil. Serpentine winding the ropes, so that they occupy small space. Each wind or turn is called a "fake."

Cordage. A generic term for all the rope of a ship.

Covering Board. A timber or plank, usually of hardwood, covering and strengthening a joint, and helping to make it watertight.

Fall. The rope that connects the blocks of a tackle, sometimes used to imply only the loose part which is pulled upon.

Fore-and-aft. In line with the keel.

Freeboard. The height of the ship above the water, when loaded.

Gear. Any part or collection of parts of a vessel's equipment, such as running-gear, boat's-gear.

Guying. Steading anything which swings. Guys are the ropes used for this purpose.

Hauling. Pulling a single rope.

Heaving. Pushing. Specifically, the act of turning about a capstan, or windlass by means of bars.

Hitch. A noose. (See Fig. II).

Hoisting. Drawing up a weight.

Hoist of a sail or flag. The part which is bent to a mast or yard or to the staff.

To Jamb. To get a rope or other body so fixed, by compression, that it cannot be moved until freed.

Kinking. The curling up of a rope when twisted too hard, or drawn unhandily from a coil.

Knot. The term applied to some hitches and to enlargements on the end of a rope.

Laniards. Chiefly the light ropes used to extend the

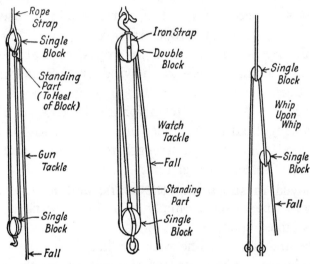

FIG. IV.—Purchases, gun tackle, watch tackle, whip upon whip.

shrouds and stays of the masts, but also used for other tying-up purposes either single or of several parts.

Lashing. A piece of rope used to fasten or secure any moveable body in a ship, or about her masts, sails and rigging.

Leading-part. The part of the tackle which is hauled upon—the fall.

Lines. Cordage smaller than rope, except when joined to another word, such as clew-lines, mooring-lines, etc.

Overhaul. To extend the several parts of a tackle, or other assemblage of ropes, communicating with blocks, or deadeyes, so that they may be again placed in a state of action. To examine.

Paint-work. Any part of the ship which is painted, particularly the deck fittings.

Port. The left hand side of the ship.

Preventer. An additional rope, to support another subjected to excessive strain.

Purchase. Any form of gearing to give additional power, such as tackles, capstans, windlass, screws, etc.

Reeving. Passing the end of a rope through any hole or channel in a block, thimble, ringbolt, etc.

To Rig. To fit the shrouds, stays, braces, etc., to their respective masts and yards.

Rigging. A general name given to all the ropes employed in supporting the spars, and to extend or reduce sail.

Ropes. All cordage in general above one inch in circumference.

Round-turn. The passing of a rope once completely round anything.

Running-rigging. That which is fitted for the purpose of arranging the sails, by passing through various blocks. All that is not standing rigging.

Setting up. Increasing the tension of the shrouds, stays and backstays, to secure the masts by tackles, laniards, etc.

To ship. To put anything in its position. Also to join a vessel as part of the crew.

Ship-shape. Correct according to the usage on ships.

Skids. Pieces of wood, across the ship on which the boats, spare spars, etc., are stowed.

Slack. Decreased tension of a rope. The part which hangs loose.

To Slue. To turn anything about.

Spars. Small trees.

Starboard. The right hand side of a vessel.

Square rigged. A term applied to those vessels which have yards at right angles with the length of the keel and lowermast.

Standing part of a rope. (in the making of knots, etc.) That part of a rope which is at rest, and is acted upon by the end.

Standing part. That part of a tackle which is made fast.

Standing-rigging. That which remains in a fixed position, to sustain the masts, yards, etc.

Stanchions. Upright props, supporting the decks, bulwarks, hand-rails, etc.

Stern. The after or hindmost part of a vessel.

Stop. Similar to a seizing, to fasten the end of one rope to another. A projection left on the upper part of the top-gallant and royal masts to prevent the rigging from slipping down.

Straps. Wreaths of rope spliced round blocks, or encircling a yard or any large rope, by which tackles, etc., may be connected to them. A strop.

Swaying. Hoisting. Particularly applied to the lower yards, topmasts and other of the heavier spars.

Tackle. A machine formed by the connection of a rope or fall with an assemblage of blocks.

Taut. Tight.

Unhandily. Clumsily. Slowly.

Whip. A small single tackle, formed by connecting the fall to a single block.

Whip-upon-whip. Formed by fixing the end of one whip upon another whip fall.

Whipping. The binding of the end of a rope, with several turns of twine or thin cord, to prevent its unlaying.

FINE WEATHER

CHAPTER II

TOOLS AND MATERIAL

THOSE starting to make this model will most likely have already a good kit of tools, but because in this book the endeavour will be to presume nothing, except handy fingers and common sense, the full list will be given.

The most useful tools are:—

Saw, light or heavy crosscut.

A fine-toothed, backed saw is useful for accurate cutting.

Carpenter's hammer.

Light hammer, such as an 00 rivetting hammer, but a 10-cent upholstery hammer will do.

Something with which to drill or bore holes $\frac{1}{4}$, $\frac{3}{16}$, and $\frac{1}{8}$ in. holes. This may be a brace and bitts, twist drills or gimlets.

Fine awl. A fine shoemaker's straight awl is best but a fine bradawl will do.

Something with which to bore holes as small as a $\frac{1}{2}''$ bank-pin. Pin twist drills are the best, of some three

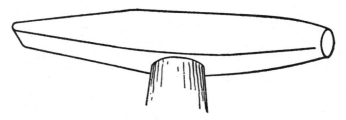

FIG. V.—A rivetter's hammer.

[16]

sizes from 75 to 40 gauge, with two chuck handles, called pin vices, to hold them. For substitutes use fine steel crochet hooks, with the ends filed to a V point.

Fretsaw or scroll saw and blades with a 10 in. bow is the best for cutting the lifts and many other small parts, but is not essential.

Chisels. At least one $\frac{1}{2}$ in., $\frac{3}{4}$, $\frac{1}{4}$ and $\frac{1}{8}$ are useful and for the very fine work on the finer model one smaller again is valuable. It can be made from a fat needle broken and ground down, from a small packing needle, but best of all from a three cornered sail needle.

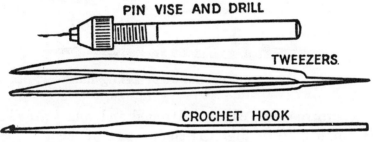

PIN VISE AND DRILL

TWEEZERS.

CROCHET HOOK

Fig. VI.—Useful small tools.

Gouges. A $\frac{1}{2}$ or $\frac{3}{4}$ in. slightly curved gouge will be found useful in shaping the hull, but is not necessary.

Spokeshaves. A small, wooden spokeshave is almost essential, in making the hull and superstructure, some prefer a drawknife. A very small one with a strong curve, comes in handy also.

Planes. A plane of from 3 to 6 in. length with a blade of about $1\frac{1}{4}$ width, is one of the most important tools. There is a gouge shaped plane about $\frac{1}{2}$ in. wide, sold by musical instrument makers which is very valuable for making concave curves; it is rather better than the gouge and concave spoke-shave, but is not so useful for work other than ship model making.

Files. A fine toothed, halfround cabinet rasp is valuable to get the sharp curves under the stern, and for all work across the grain, especially because it is indifferent to the hard and soft layers of the wood. A halfround file is better because it will give a smoother surface but is not so quick cutting.

For model B a set of die-sinker's files are very useful. There are about nine shapes of which the three-

Fig. VII.—Die-sinker's files.

cornered, fine edged, halfround and round are the most useful. Fig. VII shows some of them.

Pliers. Small pairs of edged or side cutting pliers, fine round nosed pliers (needle-nose), and square pointed pliers are needed. (See Fig. VIII.)

Cramps. A metal or wood bench-vise is most useful (see next chapter), also a few assorted small metal screw clamps,

Ordinary spring clothes pegs, with the open points cut back, are very handy for holding glued pieces together where only slight compression is necessary. Large cabinet-maker's cramps may be used to hold the hull lifts together while the glue is drying, but are not worth buying for the purpose.

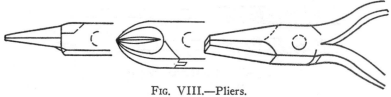

Fig. VIII.—Pliers.

Of course, a first-class pen knife (or jack knife) with a fine point.

Oil stone to keep all the tools continually sharp.

Nail set.

Fine and coarse sandpaper, with a cork rubber.

For accurate measuring and marking, there will be wanted: a scale of 12 divisions to the inch (this may be cut from the large sheet, hull plan), a straight edge, dividers, reliable square, calipers, and a B or BB and a 3H or 4H pencil.

For the rigging there will be wanted a pair of fine embroidery scissors, a few needles (No. 8, crewel, I have found the handiest, they have long eyes, easily threaded) tweezers, a medium sized crochet hook is handy for getting hold of the ends and bights of cords.

A belaying crotch is very useful, it is made from a 10 cent nut pick, by filing the point down and then filing a small nick in it. With this you can push the cord under the pins from across the model.

This appears to be quite a long list of tools, but on examination it will be found that most of them are those

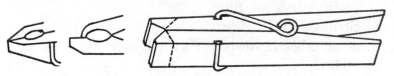

Fig. IX.—Clothes-pegs adapted for clamps.

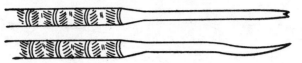

FIG. X.—A crotch for belaying ropes.

that will come in handy about the house, and that the
cost of any special ones suggested is but slight.

Those readers who have other tools which will assist
or substitute for these mentioned, will know how to use
them, and will, naturally, do so at their discretion.

LIST OF MATERIALS
For the Hull

For previous models I itemized the material required
under its mark on the plans, this, however, seems hardly
necessary because the kind and sizes are given when they
are brought into use, therefore only the bulk quantities
of everything necessary will be given here, so that when
shopping the whole outfit may be purchased at once or as
occasion offers.

White Pine for lifts. Dressed $\frac{1}{2}''$ to $\frac{5}{12}''$. Enough to
make six lifts $3\frac{1}{2}''$ by 20''. A piece $\frac{1}{4}''$x3''x5'' for H.
and one $\frac{7}{8}''$x3''x5'' for G. Or say a plank about
$6'$x$\frac{5}{12}''$x10''. The waste from this will be sufficient
for other soft-wood parts.

Rattan cane. $\frac{1}{16}''$x$\frac{1}{8}''$x11''.

Strip of $\frac{1}{8}''$x$\frac{1}{8}''$x18'' hard or semi-hard wood.

Strip $\frac{3}{16}''$x$\frac{3}{16}''$x4'' ditto.

Strip $\frac{1}{16}''$x$\frac{1}{8}''$x6'' ditto.

Oak or other hardwood $\frac{3}{4}''$x5''x18'' for base and uprights.

Dowel sticks. 1.$\frac{1}{4}''$; 2.$\frac{3}{16}''$; 3.$\frac{1}{8}''$. (Full measurement.)

Holly, box or gum wood, a small piece to make the blocks, bumkins, fife-rails, etc., may well be made of this also.

Cord. 13 yards heavy, 18 yards medium, 10 yards light, all black, and 22 yards light, buff-white. All the cord used should be of linen thread, tightly laid, such as fishing line. The heavy should be 16 to 18 thread, according to the make, which is about as thick as a No. 20 wire, or say 5 leaves of this book; the medium should be a shade more than half that thickness and the thin grade not more than half the thickness of the medium, or about No. 30, gauge.

A few feet No. 20 brass wire, Ditto copper wire, and some very thin wire.

About 100 small beads. 3 flat beads for trucks.

Bank pins, $\frac{1}{2}''$. Ordinary pins.

Needles. 4 No. 3; 2 No. 4. For outriggers.

Celluloid, about $\frac{1}{16}''$ thick x$3\frac{1}{4}''$x$2\frac{1}{2}''$.

Nails, finishing, $\frac{3}{8}''$ and $\frac{3}{4}''$.

Toothpicks, a few, round.

Sewing cotton, black 1 spool No. 24. 1 spool No. 50.

Chain. 22″ heavy. 36″ light. The heavy chain should have about 12 links to the inch, and the light about 25 links to the inch.

Silk for flags.

Lead, brass, or copper for anchors.

Glue.

Sandpaper, $1\frac{1}{2}$ to 00.

Paints: White, black, green or red, brown, gilt.

Varnish, and stain, or varnish-stain.

Black shellac.

The woodworker will find some of this in his scrap heap and will possibly have the wire, nails, etc., handy. The pine, dowel sticks, and wood for the base can be had at almost any lumber-yard, the cord comes from a fishing tackle store, silk, thread, etc., from the notion counter or someone's work basket, glue, wire nails, etc., from the hardware store, rattan cane from a chair mender, celluloid from a notion counter in the form of an ornament or fine-toothed comb; beads from a bead supply house or sometimes at a notion counter, perhaps from an old bead bag; bank pins are sold at a good stationery store.

Chain may sometimes be found at a notion counter in the form of lavelliers, if not there, then at a jewellers or as eye glass chains.

The whole outfit will cost but a few dollars, but to get it together means quite a bit of scouting round, and almost invariably one has to buy much more than one needs.

To cut out this waste of time and effort, for those whose time is of any value or whose shopping hours are limited, the publisher of this book has arranged with the author to supply complete construction sets of just the right material as specified above, with the exception of the paint, so that those who desire them, will have everything in a carton on their work bench, with the heavy cutting, casting of anchors, and so forth, done.

These sets are for the simplified model A, only, because those making the more elaborate one, will severally be working to several different scales, which would mean a different sized set for each purchaser, thus adding to their cost of production. Those making model B to the scale of $\frac{1}{12}$ in. to the foot, will find that these construction sets, being accurate to scale, will serve their purpose equally well, up to the point where they start making fine fittings and for that but little material is required—only work.

RUNNING   LIGHT BREEZE

CHAPTER III

MAKING THE HULL

THERE are several methods by which the hull can be made, it can be built up of framework and planks, as with a real ship; it can be made in layers, cut to shape as with a builder's model; or it can be cut from a solid block.

The first plan is the best, but requires a lot of skill and time; the last plan is the easiest if one has had, in this work, practise enough to ensure ones getting correct lines from drawings; the middle plan is, however, but little more trouble and is much more certain in action and, with reasonable care, it ensures the hull being correct.

That the hull shall be right is the most vital process in the whole of the model making, because all the work which follows will be but wasted on an unshapely hull.

Also, the hull itself, whether in the real ship or its model, is a thing of great beauty of line. It was stated of this clipper, that one could not lay a walking-stick to any part of her hull so that it would touch at all points, which means that every part was curved, throughout its length, breadth and depth.

You will note, as the work proceeds, that these long flowing curves are beautiful—if you have a lump, bump, dent, or anything that is not smooth and graceful then you have made a mistake.

Therefore, the second method is the one that will be adopted here, because by it I can best help you to make a correctly shaped hull.

The scale, it will be remembered, is $\frac{1}{12}$ in. to the foot throughout.

On the large sheet in the pocket at the end of the book you will find that on the SHEER PLAN there are indicated six layers, (called lifts) marked A, B, C, D, E, F, each is $\frac{5}{12}$ in. thick by rather less than 20 in. long and from the BREADTH PLAN, you will see that these same lifts come within $4\frac{1}{2}$ in. wide.

To make these, which is the first job, get some $\frac{1}{2}$ in. white pine, which usually, when machine planed for sale, comes exactly to the $\frac{5}{12}$ in. required. If you cannot get this thickness get some not less in thickness and plane it down. The lowest lift (A) is only $\frac{4}{12}$ in. thick and should be planed to this before assembling.

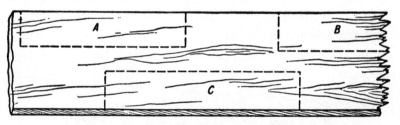

FIG. XI.—Showing how the lifts may be got from a knotty board.

Clear white pine is the best, but a board with knots in it may be used, if sufficient is obtained so that you can get the six pieces out of it between the knots and with straight grain.

In either case saw out your six pieces rectangular, pile them up, squeeze them together and see if they lie snugly face to face and if the total width is the same as that on the plan, of $2\frac{5}{12}$ in. and if the width is the same on both sides; if it is not then one or more is of uneven width.

Having got them all correct in this respect, from the breadth plan, mark one of the outlines on each; your

[25]

midship line right round the piece, and the construction lines I to XIII on the face.

These lines can most easily be transferred to the wood by pinning the plan on the wood, with a piece of typewriter carbon paper between, then tracing them with a hard sharp pencil, which is better than a stylus, which does not mark, because it shows you at once if you have run off the desired line. The very cautious person will however prefer to trace the lines onto tracing paper and to paste that onto the wood. The construction lines will however have to be on the wood itself, because the paper must be washed off later.

Anyhow, having got your lines correctly on the wood, cut the pieces out, with a fretsaw, for preference, though it can be done with a compass saw. Leave the line clearly showing on the required piece; your sawcut may wabble out but never inside the line, then sandpaper the edges until they are smooth curves with the lines only just showing.

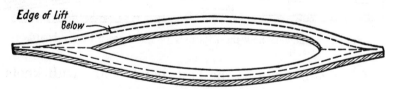

Edge of Lift
Below

Fig. XII.—One of the lifts hollowed out.

The sheer plan shows these lifts with sufficient length to include the stem and sternpost, it is better to cut these off and fit those parts separately but we will come to that later; leave them on meanwhile.

To lighten the model and make of it a hollow one, which is better and less liable to warp, pieces B, C, D, E may have their centers cut out with the fretsaw. To do this, on the under side of these pieces mark the outline of the piece that goes below, for example on the underside of B mark the outline of A and cut out to within $\frac{1}{4}$ in. of that line. This is because when the hull is finally shaped the lower edge of each piece will coincide with the upper of the next below.

Leave plenty of wood at both ends, especially under the counter where a lot is to be cut away outside.

Carry the ends of the construction lines over the edges being specially careful that the midship lines are correctly placed and vertical.

Now glue all these pieces together so that the vertical lines at the ends and sides coincide to form straight lines.

Any kind of glue may be used: casein glue, sometimes called cold-water, waterproof, or aeroplane glue is the best; it takes longer to set, but is waterproof, gives one a little more time to work and goes on thin and smooth, but it must be mixed fresh the day it is used; cabinet maker's hot glue holds well and is quite satisfactory if handled rightly, but liquid fish glue will do quite well, as the joints are to be protected by paint, use it thin and spread it with a stiff brush.

I have found that the simplest way to get all the lifts glued together in one operation without chance of their slipping askew, is to lightly nail each to the next as glued, but be careful that no nail-heads project and prevent the next lift from sitting tightly on the one below. The nailing should be done on the inside and if the lifts are hollow the points should slope to the center so that they cannot project when the outside corners are shaved off.

Another method is to clamp all the parts together and bore through them all (but not quite through the lower one) and in the hole insert a soft-wood dowel. This makes a good job because the dowels help to keep the lifts together and to prevent warp, but it can only be done with the solid model or at the extreme ends of the hollow one. The dowels should come under the after hatch and forward deck house (in the solid model) to prevent the ends from showing. In putting the parts together with dowels they are glued into the lower lift and the others are dropped on, glued as before.

If preferred, before putting on the top lift (F) the projecting corners inside may be shaved down, thus making the hull that much more hollow.

When the lifts are glued together place the whole in clamps or under heavy weights for at least 12 hours, to allow the glue to set. Glue takes longer to set thoroughly and is better if left for 24 hours.

Now mark the sheer or curve of the deck from the deck line on the sheer plan along the edges of lift F and shave the wood down to this line. A flat spokeshave is the best for doing this, but it can be done with a wide chisel. Note that this line only starts $\frac{1}{2}$ in. abaft line III, and from there curves to between X and XI from which, to the stern it rises in a straight line. The deck should be given a cambre, that is it should be a full $\frac{1}{16}$ in. higher in the center than at the edges. When cutting allow enough to sandpaper it up nice and smooth.

It is a good plan to now mark in the seams between the deck planks. There would actually be 30 planks to the inch, but about 10 to the inch will suit our purpose. They may be marked with a very sharp, hard pencil, and must run, evenly spaced, truly in line with the keel. The fore-and-aft, midship line should be quite accurate for a starting point, and should be marked a little heavier than the others.

From pieces of scrap pine cut the pieces G and H, for the poop and forecastle decks. The outline of both will be seen in the breadth plan and the thickness in the sheer

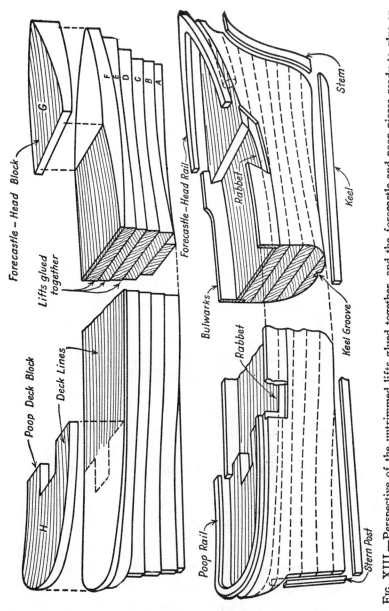

Forecastle – Head Block

G

F
E
D
C
B
A

Lifts glued
together

Poop Deck Block

Deck Lines

H

Forecastle – Head Rail

Rabbet

Bulwarks

Rabbet

Poop Rail

Stern

Keel

Keel Groove

Stern Post

FIG. XIII.—Perspective of the untrimmed lifts glued together, and the forecastle and poop pieces ready to glue on.
FIG. XIV.—Perspective of the lifts shaped, the bulwarks in position and other parts ready to place.

plan. The former (G) is a full $\frac{1}{4}$ in. thick, it has a square cut out of it to take the deck house, P. The forecastle runs from the same thickness at the after end to $\frac{11}{16}$ in. forward; both project considerably from lift F, to allow for the overhang. The upper surfaces, or decks of these pieces should have the same cambre as the main deck.

Glue and lightly nail these in position, where the nails will not show, as under the skylights and catheads. Before cutting them read the note on page 34.

Mark in the deck planks.

Now trace one of each of the XIII lines, on the BODY PLAN, onto square pieces of thin cardboard, and cut

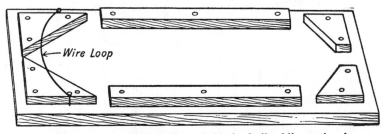

FIG. XV.—A makeshift cradle to hold the hull while cutting it.

them out to make templets, marking on each the position of the top edge of lift D.

If you have a bench vise, place the block in it with the edges up, if you have no vise, then it is worth while to make a rough cradle to lay the model in for the next operation. Fig. XV shows this; it is a stout piece of plank, with triangular blocks some $1\frac{1}{2}$ or more inches thick nailed at the ends with a heavy strip at the sides. These are adjusted to allow the model to lie comfortably in the hollow. At one end firmly fasten a stout wire loop just long enough to slip over the end of the model and hold that end down while working on the other.

This wire should be wound with a piece of cloth for padding, and a thickness or two of cloth should be laid in the cradle, under the model block during the later stages of cutting. White pine is easily bruised and should also be protected when in the bench vise, a piece of heavy sandpaper is as good as anything for this purpose; a thin piece of wood such as the lid of a cigar-box should be used to protect the deck.

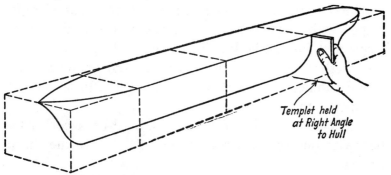

Templet held
at Right Angle
to Hull

FIG. XVI.—Perspective showing a templet held to the hull.

Having got it solidly fixed in either manner, proceed to shave off the lower corners of the lifts, down to the upper corners of the lifts below, and while doing this hold the templets to the hull in their respective positions, until by gradually shaving down, after the first rough wood is off, they fit snugly to the wood. Do not attempt to fit them one at a time, but bring all the midship part of the hull down to its marks together, and then the ends.

Note that the hull lines are convex amidships and at the upper part of the stern, and concave (hollow) at the ends, lower end astern and right up at the bow.

The templets should be held to the hull, so that the mark on them is at the top edge of lift D, with their outside edge vertical, or horizontal when the model is lying down, and they are at a right angle to the line of the keel.

The rounding of the lowest lift and the final cutting at the ends is best done with the block lying bottom up. As it is more easy to get at and to see that both sides are alike, this being even more important than that the lines are exactly to the templets, especially at the ends, and can best be judged by holding the hull directly in line with the light, so that the shadows are even on both sides and then looking at it with one eye.

The shaving can be done with a light plane, amidships, helped with a spokeshave, from there on use the spokeshave and for the hollow lines a wide shallow gouge or a spokeshave with an outward curve and finally a half-round cabinet rasp, leaving always just a little for the sandpaper to smooth up.

The sandpaper should always be used on a cork rubber, with one rounded corner for getting into the sharp curves.

Under the counter (stern) will need careful manipulation, especially from line XIII. The block has to taper to the thickness of the sternpost from some way forward at the bottom and more and more quickly as one works up, then from near the middle of E it starts to round out quickly until you get the full width of the transom, which is in three straight lines vertically, but rounded horizontally. This will explain itself as you work. It is here particularly that the rasp will be needed.

Stern and Sternpost

With regard to the stem and sternpost which come next: they may be in one with the body of the hull, in which case make templets of the outer vertical lines, from the sheer plan, and cut your stem and stern very carefully to them.

I prefer, however, to make templets also of the rabbet lines, which is where the planks are supposed to join these posts, and to cut my hull to them, having the ends flat $\frac{3}{16}$ in. across. Then from the sheer plan cut a stem and sternpost and glue and nail them on.

Keel

For the keel, cut a groove along the bottom of the hull, $\frac{5}{32}$ wide by $\frac{1}{32}$ deep. Into this glue and nail a strip of wood $\frac{5}{16}$ deep by the same width. (See K. Sheer Plan.) This will extend under the sternpost and stem, the curve of the latter being continued in an even sweep to the bottom of the keel. Now with chisel and sandpaper see that the ends of the block come nicely to the end posts.

The processes described so far, apply equally to the simplified model or to the more elaborate one, on whatever scale one is working, and if they have been carefully done, a very beautiful hull should have emerged from the block of wood.

Bulwarks

For the bulwarks of the simplified model cut a rabbet in each side of the hull $\frac{3}{32}$ in. deep, and extending $\frac{3}{16}$ in. down, in length from the lines 1 to 1, that is about $\frac{3}{4}$ in. into the poop and forecastle. Into these rabbets neatly fit pieces of white pine a full $\frac{3}{32}$ in. thick by about $\frac{3}{4}$ in. wide. Glue and lightly nail them to the hull and the poop and forecastle. The forward end may need steaming to twist it to the flare of the bow, they should project above the forecastle and poop $\frac{1}{8}$ in. and from those points be shaved down to the top sheer line shown in the sheer plan. The bulwark construction may also be seen in Fig. XIV. Sandpaper them on the outside to meet the line of the hull. Note the quick dip between the forecastle and the foremast.

Rails

The line of the bulwark has to be continued right round the poop and forecastlehead, rising from the $\frac{1}{8}$ in. at which the main parts of the bulwarks finished off to just a shade more right aft and about $\frac{3}{16}$ in. forward. The best way to make these rails is to take a piece of $\frac{3}{16}$ pine $4\frac{1}{2}$ in. long by $3\frac{1}{2}$ in. wide for the poop, lay this on the poop and draw a line round; $\frac{3}{32}$ in., inside this draw another line; fretsaw the center out and cut away the outside waste to about $\frac{3}{8}$ of this line. (See Fig. XIV.) Glue this on the poop and nail it down with bank pins, with their heads cut off, when the glue is dry shave off the waste to the line of the hull, maintaining the outward flare at the stern, then with a small chisel or pocket-knife cut the inside of this rail to the required thickness and slope at the stern.

The forecastle rail may be made in two pieces in similar fashion, being careful here also to preserve the flare, which is extreme at this point.

The joints with the bulwarks must be neatly made and should be on a bevel so that a pin point can be driven through both and into the deck.

Note: Instead of making these poop and forecastle rails from separate pieces of wood, they may be in one with the hull parts, by having G and H the necessary amount thicker and cutting down the insides of them to the deck level, thus leaving the extra wood at the sides for the rails. If you can chisel and scrape the enclosed decks nice and smooth, this is perhaps the better plan.

For model B the poop will be the same as for model A,

with the addition of a light covering-board and moldings along the front edges.

Bulwarks

For model B the forecastlehead and bulwarks will have to be more particularly made. Fig. XVII gives graphically the construction of the bulwarks. They may be built from the deck level only, by laying a covering-board (waterways) on the deck, to the level of the hull and building up from that, but a neater, easier and stronger job, on a small scale, is got by making the bulwarks as

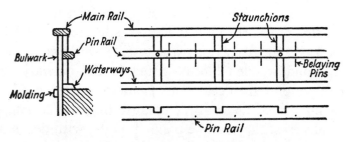

FIG. XVII.—Details of carefully made bulwarks. Scale 1/8″.

before described, but only $\frac{1}{16}$ in. thick and of a length to extend from the poop, as before, right to the extreme bow, which will necessitate a wider as well as longer piece of wood, and the cutting of a narrower rabbet in the hull to that point.

Put them temporary in position (with thumb tacks) and mark on the inside, the edge of the deck; along the middle portion true up the top $\frac{1}{16}$ in. lower than the plan indicates. From the poop to the forecastle glue on strips of wood about $\frac{1}{16}$ in. sq. vertically, about $\frac{1}{2}$ in. apart, from a line $\frac{1}{16}$ in. above the deck line to the top edge, the latter points being arrived at exactly by cutting them a shade long and then filing them down to that line.

These are the timberheads or stanchions. Now take a strip $\frac{1}{8}$ in. or a shade more by $\frac{1}{16}$ in. of a length to go from G to H, lay this on the stanchions and notch it to fit over each, then glue this, the main rail, onto the bulwark, over the stanchions, with its top edge $\frac{1}{3}$ the distance from the top edge of the bulwark, and with a pin point, nail through the three parts at every third staunchion.

From the foremast forward the bulwarks may need steaming to bring them round with a flare.

Forecastle Deck

Still keeping them in position, make and fit the parts to go under and through the forecastle deck. (See Fig. XIX.) At the two after corners will be lockers, these are small solid wooden blocks, fitted to the bulwarks and extending onto the deck about $\frac{3}{16}$ in. to which they should be firmly glued and nailed, because they are to support the bulwarks, they can be painted white, with doors outlined on the after ends. In the bow, bore a $\frac{1}{4}$ in. hole to take the bowsprit, the top edge of the hole will be almost at the top edge of the bulwark, the downward angle can be seen in the sheer plan. The safest way to make this is to mark it carefully and with the bulwarks apart cut the two half circles, with a small gouge or penknife. Now make the bowsprit to the directions given on page 87 and nail it to the deck.

On either side of the bowsprit, as far forward as possible, bore holes in the main deck and in them insert $\frac{1}{8}$ in. square sticks, to extend upwards a shade above the level of the bulwarks, pointing forward at an angle of 15 degrees. Behind these I advise gluing wedge shaped blocks, somewhat similar to the lockers, to help support the bulwarks, or if preferred one piece right across the

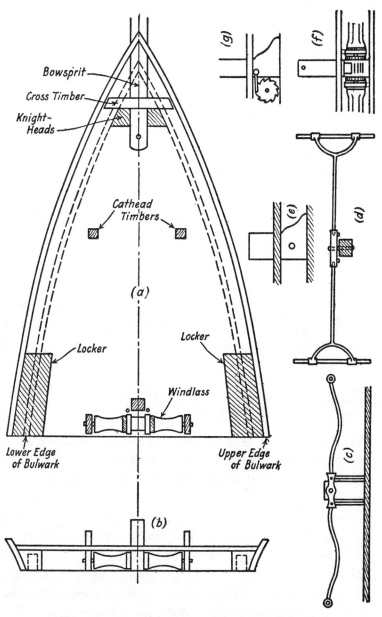

Bowsprit

Cross Timber

Knight-
Heads

Cathead
Timbers

(a)

Locker

Locker

Windlass

Lower Edge
of Bulwark

Upper Edge
of Bulwark

(b)

(g)

(f)

(e)

(d)

(c)

FIG. XIX.—Forward deck details.   Scale 1/12″.
FIG. XX.—To the right.   Windlass details.

[37]

deck. They should really be knees, or grown angle timbers, but will not show anyhow. Put in the cross-timber, touching both bulwarks, the knight-heads and the bowsprit.

The bulwarks should now be removed and painted white inside, except where they are to be glued, because glue sticks so much better to the raw wood. The rail and stanchions can be varnished a mahogany color. When dry the bulwarks may be permanently nailed and glued to the hull, and to each other at the bow.

From a piece of $\frac{1}{16}$ in. white pine, cut a deck to fit between them at the level indicated for the solid piece G, cutting holes in it to allow the timber-heads in the bow (knight-heads) and the bowsprit to project. Cut three holes for the heads of the windlass posts to project, marking their positions on the deck below, as in Fig. XIX. Now remove this deck, mark the deck planks on it and lay it aside.

Windlass

The design of the windlass can be seen in Fig. XX. It is composed of two wooden barrels for winding in the anchor cables, suspended on four posts, two long at the ends and two short in the middle, between these two latter, there is an iron barrel with teeth to engage a pawl suspended from the center "Samson" post, to prevent the windlass barrels from working back. To the top of this post, above the deck, is hinged a long bar with cross handles at the ends. The "pumping" up and down of these handles turns the barrels, through rods with pawls at the ends catching other teeth on the windlass. Erect this in position.

Spurling-Gates

Just abaft the windlass barrels are holes in the deck, called the "spurling-gates." After the cables have been round the barrels, these holes lead them to the chain lockers below.

Hawse-pipes

The hawse-pipes are $\frac{3}{16}$ in. holes in both bows, $\frac{3}{4}$ in. abaft the stem and $\frac{1}{4}$ in. below the lower molding. They

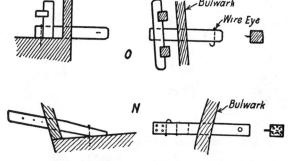

FIG. XXI.—Cathead and bumkin. Scale 1/12".

are best seen in rigging plan. They point up and emerge in line with the windlass barrels. For the simplified model they need be only $\frac{1}{4}$ in. deep. The angle of their entrance gives them the oval appearance.

Glue on the forecastle deck, putting a, not too heavy, weight on it until the glue is set.

Erect a stout (about 8 in.) turned stanchion at the after edge of this deck to support it in the middle.

Catheads

The catheads had better come next, because they help to retain this deck. For both models A and B they are a full $\frac{1}{8}$ in. square by 1 in. long, half of which projects.

[39]

(See deck plan.) Bevel the inboard end to lie flat on the deck when the piece points up slightly. In the outer half bore three small holes fore-and-aft, and at the extreme end four vertically in a square formation. Cut a square hole in the bulwarks to fit so that they will point slightly upwards, push them through with a touch of glue and nail to the deck.

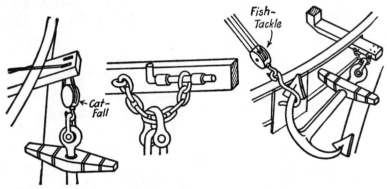

Fig. XXII.—Catting and fishing the anchor. Chain stopper.

Cathead-butts

For model B, in line with the inside ends of the catheads, cut $\frac{1}{8}$ in. square holes; through these push posts of the same size long enough to touch the deck below and project $\frac{3}{16}$ in. above. These are to take the strain of "catting the anchor" and to lash the flukes to, when at sea.

Catting the anchor is hoisting it up by the ring, from the edge of the hawse-pipe to the end of the cathead. The holes we bored in the end of the cathead (of which there should really be six) representing sheaves or pulleys, equallying a three-fold block. A rope is rove through these and through a large three-fold block with a hook; this is hooked into the ring of the anchor and the fall (end) is taken to the capstan, when by turning this the anchor is hove up to the cathead.

To get the crown of the anchor up, a cable is made fast to the lowermast-head, on this is a three-fold and a two-fold block-tackle. A chain with a large hook on the end is hooked into the fluke of the anchor; the tackle is hooked to this, then, by again heaving on the capstan, the crown is brought aboard or, until well away at sea, the fluke is hooked and lashed to the rail. This is called "fishing the anchor." Fig. XXII shows this action with the exception of the intervening chain and hook.

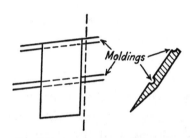

FIG. XXIII.—Sheathing, or chafing board for anchor fluke.

The fish-tackle may be shown, with the hook lashed to one of the knight-heads.

When fishing the anchor the sharp fluke is liable to tear away the moldings and bulwarks so there is a heavy sheathing plank placed where it comes up. This is shown in Fig. XXIII. It is represented by a piece of wood $\frac{3}{4}$ in. deep, $\frac{3}{8}$ wide by $\frac{3}{32}$ in. at the thickest part. It fits snugly to the ship's side, over the moldings.

So that the anchor may be quickly dropped in emergency, when in shallow or dangerous waters, the ring is hung from the cathead by a short chain, one end of which is stapled to the cathead and the other is on a slip bolt. The kind of bolt which just turns is the best, but the kind which withdraws like the bolt on a door is easier to make. It is shown on Fig. XXII. Make two staples of pins and drive them in abaft the cathead near the ship's side, about $\frac{3}{16}$ in. apart. Thread a larger pin, with the end bent over, through the inner one of these, through the link of a piece of chain about $\frac{3}{8}$ in. long, and through the other staple. When we put the anchor in position this chain reeves through the ring and staples to the cathead. The standing part of the chain, called the stopper, would be better bolted to the fore side of the cathead.

The end of the cathead usually has a cat's head carved and painted on it.

Bumkins

The bumkins are posts somewhat like the catheads, only lighter, which project from the quarters, for the main braces to hook to. (See Fig. XXI.)

They are $\frac{3}{32}$ in. sq. and $\frac{5}{8}$ in. long, of which $\frac{7}{16}$ is outboard, cut square holes in the rails to take them, and glue and nail the inner ends to the deck, $\frac{3}{8}$ in. abaft line XII. At the outer end bore a horizontal hole for the brace pennant, and for the better model (B) fasten a piece of the smallest chain to the end, underneath, stapling the other end of this to the ship's side, at the molding, so that it leads down and aft.

Moldings

Your ship will want two moldings round her, for either model. The heavy one which runs along the main deck line, immediately below it, may be of wood $\frac{1}{16}$ in. sq. with the outer edge rounded, but a piece of smooth braided cord is neater and easier. If the cord is used, glue and nail it with a pinpoint at the bow, glue it about half way along, stretch it to the stern, and lightly nail in position here and there, bring it round the counter and so to the other bow. The wooden molding will go on similarly, except that it had better be in three pieces, one for each side and another, steamed, for the stern.

The upper molding for the model A, will be a piece of thin cord, glued along the top edge of the bulwark and on the same line at the ends. For model B it will be a strip of wood, $\frac{1}{8}$ by $\frac{1}{16}$ in. glued and nailed squarely on top of the bulwarks from forecastle to poop, so that it covers them and the ends of the stanchions, and projects over the side $\frac{1}{16}$ in. It can be continued at the ends

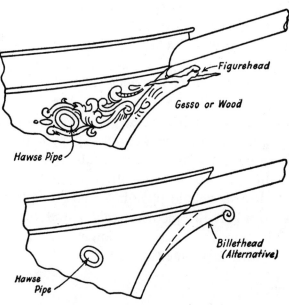

FIG. XXIV.—Figurehead, and a billethead.

with either wood or cord. They will both be best seen on the large rigging plan.

Figurehead

Both models will need a figurehead under the bowsprit this is a queen (sovereign) with one arm back along the hull to lead the ship on and the other extended to point the way. (See Fig. XXIV.) Incidentally, I am not quite sure that this was the figurehead, but I have reason to believe so, and it is quite a probable one. This may be carved in boxwood and set on the stem, or modelled in plasticine and cast in plastic wood or metal, but I made mine of gesso. I made an armature (skeleton) for it by having a long pin sticking out of the bow to where the figure's head comes, then I put in another bent one to represent the extended arm, and on these built up the figure, blocking it out roughly first, then adding here and there, and cutting away as required. I applied the gesso by filling a broken-down propelling pencil with the gesso, squeezing it out of the fine point. A sugar icing tool will do this, or even a paper bag, if the gesso is thin, but the pencil makes a fine tool. The lines of Her Majestie's streaming hair come on to the body of the hull down to and round the hawse pipes, gradually becoming decorative curls. The hawsepipe also should be given a rim or lip.

The bulwarks should have holes bored in them of $\frac{3}{32}$ in. dia. to admit the mooring cables and ropes. They are rather more than half way down and $\frac{3}{4}$ in. from the forecastle and poop on either side.

Waterways

In model B we have not quite finished fitting the bulwarks as there are yet the waterways to go in place. The ends of the staunchions should be $\frac{1}{16}$ in. up from the deck; in this space, from the locker forward to the poop, insert a strip of wood $\frac{1}{8}$ wide by $\frac{1}{16}$ in. thick, with the top outer edge rounded. Touch the under ends of the stanchions with glue and the under side of the waterways. See Fig. XVII. A nice finishing touch will be added by boring the scupper holes, these are to let the water drain off the deck. They should be three in number, one right at the lowest part of the deck between lines VII and VIII, one on line IX and one between V and VI. They start at the edge of the waterway and come out through the hull $\frac{3}{16}$ in. below the molding, they may have lips to keep the water from dribbling down the ship's side; on a model of this scale a large pin cut off short with its head flattened will serve. For a larger model they should be semicircular pieces of thin brass.

Rudder

Next comes the rudder. So many people think that the rudders of big ship models are too small that it is worth mentioning that the larger the ship the smaller, proportionately is the rudder. A rudder of the size shown is sufficient, when at an angle of 30 degrees, or hard over, to bring the ship quickly round on her heel; with a powerful worm-screw gearing it has such a leverage that when a heavy sea is running, it is all a strong man can do to move it, and it can throw two men away from the wheel when a really heavy sea catches it, as when running before the wind.

Anyhow the size and shape shown on the above plan and Fig. XXV may be taken correct, for model A the one marked a. will be sufficient. Make it of any semi-hard wood, the thickness of the sternpost, but tapering about one-third astern, bore a hole carefully under the counter to take the top (stock), cut off the heads of three $\frac{3}{8}$ in. nails, insert the blunt ends in the sternpost, and press the points into the rudder, with the bottom of the rudder level with the keel and leaving just the least gap between the hull and it.

For model B, we will have to be more particular. Fig. XXV shows how a real rudder is built and fastened. The rudder will be cut as before but without the solid stock, for this get a piece of ⅛ in. round stick, at the lower end cut a groove in it to take the rudder; point it as shown, and glue it on. On the smallest scale model it will be sufficient to cut the heads off five bank pins and bend ⅛ in. of them at a right angle; then with the round-nosed pliers make eyes just big enough to take the pin ends in five other pins; push the pins with eyes into the sternpost, evenly spaced between the end of the stock and the top of the keel; place the rudder in position and mark where the eyes come. To get the rudder in position it will be necessary to cut a groove in the top of the sternpost and a hole above that to take the rudder-stock, so that the edge of the rudder comes close to the stern-post. The corners of both rudder and post should be chamfered.

Having got your marks on the rudder, cut notches in it, and drive in the bent pins, so that they will all lie in the eyes, when the rudder is shipped. The straps, apparently holding the pintles and gudgeons in place may be simulated by gluing narrow strips of thin cardboard onto the rudder and stern, the lower edge of the pintle strap being in line with the upper edge of the gudgeon strap.

Another and rather better way to make the pintles and gudgeons is to get some very thin sheet brass, cut some of this into strips $\frac{3}{32}$ in. wide; take a piece long enough to make the straps on either side and to come round the edge of the rudder. In the middle of the strip, nip a pin with the head nearly all filed away, then bend it out and back again so that it fits snug to the rudder and holds the pin (a spot of solder will help to retain the pin). Snip the end off leaving ⅛ in. projecting down; punch two little holes in both ends of these straps, at corresponding positions, slip them on the rudder and drive a bank pin through the rudder and both straps, clinching the ends down and filing the heads flat; do this for all five pintles. Make other pieces for the gudgeons, exactly the same way, to fit on the sternpost, but when in position slip the pins out, and ship the rudder, as before. The pintles should be directly under the center of the rudder-stock, so that the whole will swing from side to side, without "throwing."

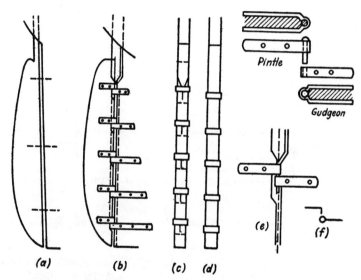

Fig. XXV.—Simplified rudder (a) with details of more exact rudder.

Channels

Both models A and B will need channels; they are wide shelf-like timbers projecting from the ship's side to spread the rigging and keep the weight off the bulwarks. (See Fig. XXVI.) Semi-hard wood is the best for them. The lower ones are $\frac{3}{16}$ in. thick, tapering to a bare $\frac{1}{8}$ in.; at the fore and main they are $2\frac{1}{4}$ in. and at the mizzen $1\frac{3}{4}$ in. long; all are $\frac{1}{4}$ in. wide. The upper channels are the same length, just a shade less in width and about half the thickness. The chains (which is the old-time name for the chains or iron bands which hold the deadeyes down) come through these, therefore they should have holes bored through them, close to their outer edges and large enough to take the rigging cord, at $\frac{3}{16}$ in. intervals, 11 at the fore and main and 9 at the

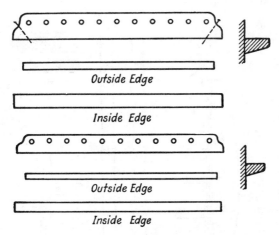

Outside Edge

Inside Edge

Outside Edge

Inside Edge

Fig. XXVI.—Lower and upper channels. (Fore and Main).

mizzen. This answers well for model A, but for B in which we are going to have deadeyes, the holes are a nuisance to work with so, make them rather larger, then with a fine knife blade split the channel, through the holes, mark the pieces split off and lay them aside carefully, to be glued on later.

Nail and glue the channels to the hull, with the forward ends level with the masts, the lower one immediately below the moldings, and the upper in line with the pin rail.

Waterline

Scratch in the waterline $\frac{1}{8}$ in. from the top edge of lift D, as shown in the sheer plan, being very careful that it is truly horizontal. It is better to mark it with a soft pencil first and then holding it up look along the line, to see that it is level.

Plank Markings

The plank markings may also be scratched in above the water line. Doing this certainly adds considerably to the

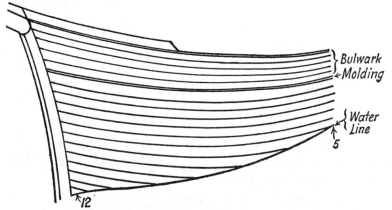

FIG. XXVII.—Markings to show the caulked joins between the planks.
Note: This being a perspective, the planks appear proportionately wider at the stem than they would viewed beam-on.

appearance of the model, but it is an awkward job and must be done well or not at all. For the bulwarks four parallel lines widening to the bow will be sufficient. For the hull it must be especially noted that the planks are not the same width all the the way along, but are wider amidships that at the ends, being about one-third narrower at the bow and $\frac{1}{2}$ at the stern but widening again under the counter. A chincher-built row boat shows the idea plainly. (See Fig. XXVII.) From the molding to the waterline, five marks amidships will be enough, this will give you 12 on line I and about 13 on line XII., from the molding to the water-line.

Across the transom the lines run parallel with the rail.

The lines need not be so closely marked so long as the direction and proportion is correct.

Painting

That finishes the building of the hull. It has to be painted now. Give the deck one coat of clear varnish, of good quality. If it dries shiny, rub it down with pumice stone and water, or a fine grade of steel wool. It is desired to keep the damp and dust out of it, but not to darken it or make it shiny. The inside of the bulwarks in model B we have already painted, those of A should have two thin coats of white paint, and then have stripes of burnt umber and burnt sienna mixed, painted on them to represent stanchions and rail, forming panels.

The insides and upper edges of the rails on the poop and forecastle should be white, but the top edge of the rail between should be black.

The outside of the hull should be given a thin coat of flat white, when dry this should be rubbed down, almost bare, with fine sandpaper; cracks or inequalities should then be filled in with putty or some thick paint from the bottom of the can. White is used for this priming coat because it has good body, but more because it clearly shows up any defects.

Below the water line can then be given two coats of a metallic green, or the appearance of copper can be simulated with yellow ochre and burnt sienna, or, if preferred, it can be painted with copper bronze paint.

Above the water line, it should receive two or three thin coats of black, the last one being applied with a small, flat hog-bristle brush, with a little brown and red run in here and there, so as not to have it too jet black or too even. After each coat, the paint must be rubbed down with fine sandpaper, using fine steel wool in the awkward curves. The last coat should be rubbed down lightly with pumicestone-powder and water, to take off the shine.

The main deck molding will be white, the black being very evenly cut to it with a fine brush.

The figurehead will be white and gold, and the scroll-work round the bows gold.

The vessel's name will have to be painted on both bows and on the transom, which will also bear her port of registry. If you can do these very neatly in white or gold that is best, if not, the name plates given on the hull plan can be cut out, glued on and varnished over.

CHAPTER IV

DECK FURNISHINGS

THE next process is to make the deck fittings; these can be made very simple, or a lot of time and fine work can be put into them.

Before starting on them it will be well to make a temporary, working base to hold the model. For this purpose get a piece of stout plank about 6 in. wide and on it erect two uprights, cut out roughly to fit the hull, from templates, III and X, make them an easy fit with a slot for the keel, and line them with a piece of cloth or felt, but be careful that the model sits upright in them with the keel level; if necessary packing up one side or shaving the bottom of them. A good plan is to bore a hole through the middle of base piece and through another piece of plank about the same size, gluing a piece of broom-stick into the lower one, long enough to project into the upper; on this "turntable" the model can be swung round as one works, saving the trouble of lifting it, or walking round it. A few thumb-tacks in the lower board help it it slide easily.

The deck fittings for the simplified model A, will first be described, but of course any of those explained later may be used.

Mast Holes

So that there may be definite points from which to measure along the deck, mark and bore the holes for the masts. When marking in the deck planks, it was advised that the midship line be marked a little heavier than the others, make sure that this is truly central. Now carefully get the position of the vertical midship line (VII) and mark where it crosses the other. One inch abaft this make a mark for the center of the main mast, punch a little hole there and bore a $\frac{1}{4}$ in. hole at the angle shown in the large rigging plan. Five and one-eighth in. forward of the midship line bore a $\frac{3}{16}$ in. hole for the foremast, at the same angle. The hole for the mizzen mast will have to wait until the cabin house is in place, as it goes through it, with a $\frac{1}{8}$ in. hole just abaft that, for the trysail mast.

From these mast holes your deck furnishings will take their positions, always being careful that they are fairly amidships.

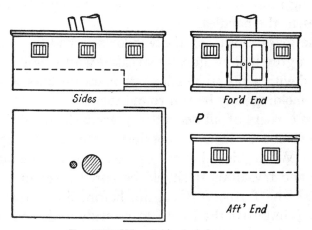

Fig. XXVIII.—Cabin deck-house.

Cabin Deck-house

The after, or cabin deck-house, sometimes called a coachhouse, may be made from an oblong block of pine $\frac{7}{12}$ in. thick, $1\frac{5}{8}$ in. long and $1\frac{1}{8}$ in. wide, or to fit snugly into the slot in the poop piece H. projecting onto the main deck $\frac{1}{2}$ in. Round the top edge of this run a cornice-molding, by gluing round it a strip of wood $\frac{1}{16}$ sq. and then with a V chisel or small file, cutting a bead. It should really be a bit wider than it is deep, and considerably so at the fore end. (See Fig. XXVIII.)

Along the lower edge there should be a covering board, or strip of wood $\frac{1}{12}$ in. deep by half that width, glued to the side of the house and the deck. This may be omitted.

On the fore end paint a double door, opening in the center, with a window on either side close up under the molding. At the sides there will be three windows and on the after end, two.

The doors were most likely all white, but they might have been teak or mahogany panelled and molded; as the former would not show at all, we will adopt the latter, by painting red-brown panels and edges, two pin-heads will represent the handles.

The glass effect for the windows is had by painting them a grey-blue diagonally streaked with white, blended in, and with white stripes down to mark the bars, a brown paint molding may be run round them.

The corners of all deckfittings are well rounded so as to hurt one as little as possible when washed against them. When this is in position, the holes for the mizzen-mast and trysail-mast should be bored through the top of it. The former to be $\frac{3}{8}$ in. before line XI and the latter $\frac{1}{8}$ in. abaft that, both to be truly midships and to slope at the right angle.

Skylight

The skylight sets in the position indicated on the deck plan. It is made from $\frac{1}{4}$ in. thick pine $\frac{1}{2}$ in. wide by $\frac{3}{4}$ in. long; it has windows recessed and painted all round it. The projecting top is a very thin piece of mahogany or cedar. The body of it is white with brown moldings and the top bright. Bright or brightwork on a ship is wood that is oiled or varnished—not painted. (See Fig. XXIX).

Companion-way

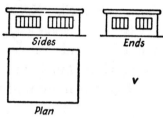

Fig. XXIX.—Skylight.

The companion-way is the means of entrance from the poop to the cabin. It has small, double-doors, facing aft, but as these are too short to allow of anyone entering without stooping, the top part has a panel which slides back, thus, when open, permitting entrance to the ladder which leads to the doors.

The body of it is made of a block of wood similar to the skylight, but $\frac{1}{16}$ in. shorter, on this is glued a thin piece of hardwood as before, and on that a wedge-shaped piece of wood, with another slip of hardwood on top, as may be seen in Fig. XXX. On the after end, in the center, the edge of the top is cut level with the block and on the filed level face of the three pieces, is painted a double door.

Steering Gear

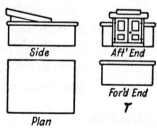

Fig. XXX.—Companion-way.

The part of the steering gear which shows on deck, is in reality a wooden drum, supported on a stout axle, turning in iron bracket supports, on the forward end of which is the "wheel." From the tiller below, a rope comes through the deck round the drum and back through the deck again to the tiller; by turning the wheel the tiller and with it the rudder is moved. Over this drum is placed a removable box, supported on legs.

All we need show is the box on legs with the axle and wheel. (See Fig. XXXI.)

A block of wood $\frac{3}{8}$x$\frac{5}{16}$x$\frac{3}{16}$ in. will form the cover. It should have the top corners, at the sides, bevelled. It can be white, but if made of the same wood as the skylight top it is more uniform. The wheel should be 5 ft. that is $\frac{1}{2}$ in. in diameter. It would really be of wood with a brass rim and center plate, but it is almost impossible to make a wooden one this size. If you can find the sprocket wheel from an old watch or clock of the right size, it serves well, with every other tooth filed away, the spokes being painted brown. The easiest way to make one is to cut it from celluloid, something less than $\frac{1}{16}$ in. thick, painting it all brown except a brass-color rim. Through the center drive a brass escutcheon pin, or thick ordinary pin, the end going into the wood block, so that the wheel stands away from it, $\frac{1}{8}$ in. It sits better with a sleeve over the axle, between the wheel and the block; this can be made of celluloid, wood or lead.

Now take four bank pins, snip the heads off and with a touch of glue or shellac place three small beads on the middle of each; bore, and drive the heads into the corners of the block and the points into the deck to form turned legs. Paint them white. The spokes of the wheel should clear the deck by about $\frac{1}{16}$ in. This sets right aft.

Binnacle

We will give her the old fashioned binnacle, which is the stand containing the mariner's compass. It is like an upright cupboard, with a door opening right across on the upper half and the usual cupboard doors below. (See Fig. XXXII.)

It is a square block of wood $\frac{5}{16}$x$\frac{5}{32}$x$\frac{5}{16}$ in. high, it has the same hardwood top as the other poop fittings and the doors and panels are painted on in the same way.

If you can, make a little bell to hang in a bracket on it, but it must be not larger than $\frac{1}{16}$ in. high or wide, and should be hung in a wire loop or staple, and painted bronze color.

Lazarette Hatch

To one side of the binnacle there should be a hatch $\frac{1}{4}$ in. sq. and $\frac{1}{12}$ in. high, this leads to the lazarette where the stores are kept.

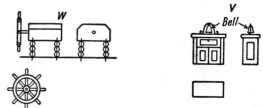

Fig. XXXI.—Steering-gear.   Fig. XXXII.—Binnacle.

Deck House

On the main deck there is a house in which are the galley (kitchen) and crew quarters. It is shown in Fig. XXXIII and its position is indicated on the deck plan.

It is made from a block of pine the same height as the after deck house, $3\frac{3}{4}$ in. long by $1\frac{3}{8}$ in. wide. It has three doors on each side, opening at their forward edge, and three windows; at the after end there are two windows. It has a molding round the top edge and a covering-board at the bottom, all of which are similar to those on the after deckhouse. Between the doors it is panelled.

Forward Boats

On top of this house there are two boats, keel up. They are glued down to two skids.

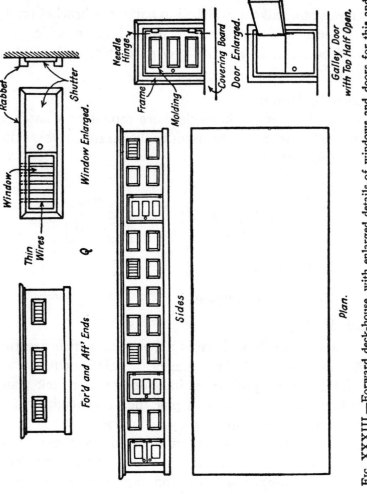

Rabbet

Shutter

Window

Window Enlarged.

Thin Wires

Q

For'd and Aft' Ends.

Needle Hinge

Frame

Molding

Covering Board

Door Enlarged.

Galley Door with Top Half Open.

Sides

Plan.

Fig. XXXIII.—Forward deck-house, with enlarged details of windows and doors for this and the cabin-house.

Boats and skids can be of pine and will be painted white.

The boats are similar to those shown in Fig. XLIII, and the skids are seen in Fig. XXXIV.

Ladders

A ladder will be wanted on each side, leading to the poop and forecastle decks. (Fig. XXXV) As the height of these decks is only three feet, two steps on each will be sufficient. They can be made from $\frac{1}{32}$x$\frac{1}{16}$ in. hardwood, cedar or the like, with their sides on a bevel so that they lie against the edge of the deck. If their lower ends are left a bit long they can be driven into the deck, which

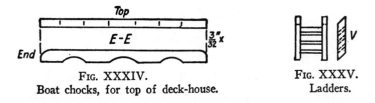

FIG. XXXIV.
Boat chocks, for top of deck-house.

FIG. XXXV.
Ladders.

will aid the glue to hold them in position. An easier and better way is to cut them with the fretsaw in one piece from celluloid, not less than $\frac{1}{16}$ in. thick. There should also be another ladder from the poop deck to the top of the cabin-house.

After Hatch

The after hatch between lines VIII and IX is shown in Fig. XXXVI. It is a block of pine $\frac{3}{16}$ high by $\frac{3}{4}$ by $\frac{3}{4}$ in. wide. The edge has a shallow groove in it, the top bulge being the tarpaulins (canvas covers) and the lower the covering board. At the after end is a scuttle similar to that on the companion hatch aft, but with the doors extending only down to the hatch proper. It will be painted black with brightwork doors and top to the scuttle. This latter was to admit emigrants who lived in the after 'tweendecks.

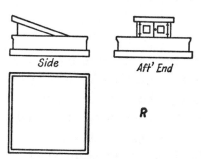

FIG. XXXVI.—After hatch.

Main Hatch

The main hatch is the same height, width and shape. It has no scuttle and is painted black.

Main Fife-rail

Posts and rails, called fife-rails, are required at the fore and main masts (ships sometimes had them at the mizzen also). They are fitted with belaying-pins for the running gear. (See Fig. XXXVIII.)

At the main there are two $\frac{1}{8}$ in. sq. posts, let into square holes in the deck and there glued, standing above it $\frac{5}{12}$ in. high. These set $\frac{3}{12}$ in. forward of the mast, center to center, and the same distance on either side. They are joined athwartships by a strip $\frac{1}{8}$ in. width by rather less in depth. From their fore sides extend other rails $\frac{1}{8}$x$\frac{1}{16}$ in. supported at the ends by having bank-pins driven through them, with beads to represent the turnings. These

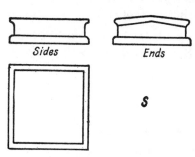

FIG. XXXVII.—Main hatch.

should be glued and nailed to the uprights with pin-points. The athwart piece and side pieces should have four holes, with half bank-pins in each, to represent belaying-pins.

The wood should be bright and the beads painted white.

Forward Fife-rail

At the foremast there is another fife-rail, with posts of the same dimensions set in the deck, at positions corresponding with those at the main. The construction is the same, except that the fore-and-aft rails are $\frac{5}{8}$ in. long and are glued to the forward end of the deckhouse, without stanchions. (See Fig. XXXIX.)

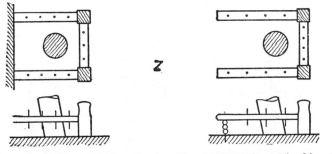

FIG. XXXIX.—Forward fife-rail.   FIG. XXXVIII.—Main fife-rail.

Bitt-heads

Four sets of bitts will be wanted, one for either side on the main deck, set close to the waterways, almost abreast at the foremast, and one on either side on the poop, set across the inner ends of the bumkins. Their construction may be seen in Fig. XL and the positions on the deck plan. The posts are $\frac{1}{8}$ in. sq. of hard or semi-hardwood, standing $\frac{3}{8}$ in. above the deck, with about $\frac{3}{16}$ in. sunk into the deck and glued. The bolsters or cross bars, are $\frac{5}{8}$x$\frac{1}{8}$x$\frac{1}{16}$ in. and are recessed into the bitts. They may be dark brightwork or painted white. There should, by rights, be another set on either side at line X. The

[61]

mooring ropes are made fast to these in harbor. Some ships did not have the bolsters and some had iron bitts.

Galley Funnel

Between the boats at about $\frac{1}{2}$ in. from the after end of the house there will be the funnel for the galley stove as shown in Fig. XLI. It is just a round stick $\frac{1}{16}$ in. dia. and $\frac{5}{10}$ in. high, the top $\frac{1}{8}$ in. is a shade bigger, to represent a revolving cowl. It is glued into the house top, and painted black.

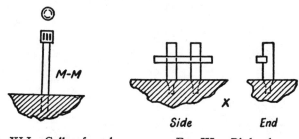

FIG. XLI.—Galley funnel.   FIG. XL.—Bittheads.

Capstan

The capstan shown in Fig. XLII can be made from a piece of dowel stick or pine. It has six holes bored in the top edge to take the capstan bars, and is fastened to the deck by having a long pin driven right through it. It may be painted black or green. A vessel of this size would probably have had another capstan on the main deck, between the mainmast and main hatch. This may be put on if desired.

Windlass posts

On the simplified model we have not the complete windlass, so the posts apparently coming from it will have to be made and fixed in the deck. The forward one of the

[62]

three (the samson post) is $\frac{5}{16}$ high by a full $\frac{1}{8}$ in. sq., the other two are $\frac{3}{16}$ high, by $\frac{1}{8}$x$\frac{1}{16}$ in. sq. all are pointed and glued into the deck. If desired a small nail may be driven into the samson post near the top, abaft, round this twist a small piece of copper wire, extend the ends horizontally $\frac{1}{4}$ in. bend them down sharply and stick the ends in the deck, this is to represent the leverage gear, described in the previous chapter. The ends of the knightheads and cathead-posts need not be shown. For their position see the deck plan.

Bell

At the after edge of the forecastle deck there should be a big bell, (big in reality, that is). All ships carry two bells, one aft, or on the bridge nowadays, and another forward. The after bell was struck every half-

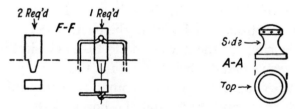

Fig. XLII.—Simple capstan and windlass posts.

hour by the man at the wheel on American ships and by one of the apprentices on watch, on British ships. It was struck once for each half-hour of the watch of four hours, thus two bells would be five, nine or one o'clock, and eight bells (the finish of the watch) eight, twelve or four o'clock. This bell was answered by the forward bell being struck by the lookout man. The latter bell had to be large because it was also used as a warning signal by ships at anchor.

[63]

On our ship it would be about ⅛ in. deep by the same diameter at the mouth. It should be hung from a wire bracket. Bronze is the right color for it.

The after bell was mentioned with the binnacle.

After Boats

There should be a boat hung in davits on either quarter, between the main rigging and the poop. One of these should be square sterned and the other of the whaleboat type, their shape may be seen in the deck plan and in Fig. XLIII. They should be hollowed out and have the thwarts (seats) in place, with such other gear as you care to make, oars, masts, sails, etc., for example. At each end drive in a bentover-pin hook.

The davits may be made from No. 20 brass wire; the end being turned over to make a ring, the wire then bent to a curve with the other end driven into a hole bored in the edge of the bulwark, these holes being just a shade farther apart than the hooks in the boat.

To the rings of the davits and to the hooks in the boats fasten very small double blocks (for the making of these see next chapter). Reeve some of your thin cord through these and thus hang the boats, with their keels just below the top edge of the bulwarks, now take the ends of the tackles pass then under the boats and hitch them to the opposite davit, thus bousing the boat in to the davit, so that it will not swing about. Take another cord, hitch it to the rings of the davits, to be tight when the boat falls (tackles) are vertical, take the ends down and fasten them off to the main and mizzen chains.

All the boats should be white with brown gunwhales, or top planks.

These boats had better be left to one side until the rigging is completed.

Taffrail

This handrail round the poop is, perhaps, the most delicate piece of work in the whole ship. It is important that it should be neat because it is prominent.

It is shown on the deck plan and in Fig XLIV. It can be made from three pieces of hardwood, joining them with half-laps, about 1 in. abaft the bumkins, so as to get

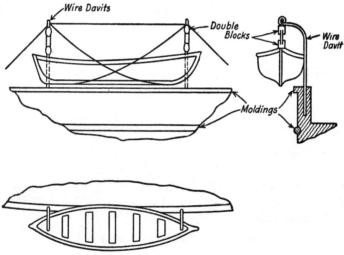

FIG. XLIII.—The after boats, in davits.

some of the curve on each. It can be made in one piece from $\frac{1}{16}$ in, three-ply wood, if obtainable. I, however, found the most satisfactory way was with a strip of rattan cane, such as is used by upholsterers for fastening in position the cane bottoms of chairs. This splits readily with a blunt knife, and can be planed and sandpapered to the desired dimensions of a bare $\frac{1}{8}x\frac{1}{16}$ in. A piece 11 in. long is required.

Lay this on the poop rail, but to overhang at the stern enough to preserve the overhang line there. It may need a little steaming to bend round the stern nicely. Mark the midship position at the stern and the position of the bumkins, between these marks make two others on either side, and from there, forward, at $\frac{3}{4}$ in. intervals. At each of these marks bore a very small hole through into the rail below. Now file the heads of some bank pins flat and push one through each hole; on these drop beads to build up to a full $\frac{1}{8}$ in. (most likely using three). Put a drop of glue or shellac on each, to retain them in position; turn it over and lightly hammer the pin points into position. The rail should be painted white and the beads brown to represent bright, turned, wooden posts.

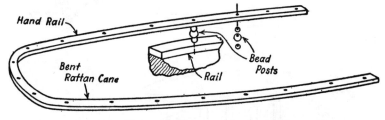

FIG. XLIV.—Taffrail or monkey-rail.

The low poop is frequently called the "monkey poop" and the rail round is the "monkey-rail."

Eye-bolts

Staples will be needed in the deck, for the fore and main stays and for the halliards. Their position is shown on the deck plan. They should be of No. 20 brass wire, $\frac{3}{8}$ to $\frac{1}{2}$ in. long, and those for the stays should be set into the deck at an angle so that they will not draw out. Small screw-eyes are better if you can get them the right size. Two similar staples will be wanted in the stem, for the bobstays, others under the lower molding, in line with the catheads, and another on each side half an inch forward of that, above the molding, for the jib-stays and bowsprit shrouds.

SCUDDING.

CHAPTER V

ELABORATED DECK FURNISHINGS

THE deck fittings for the more elaborate model B, will be of the same dimensions as those given in the previous chapter, but will be more carefully finished in detail.

The parts as they would be on a real ship will be described; it is for you to get as near to that as you can, to which end some suggestions will be offered. The nearer you get to the real thing the better your model, but there are many small details and methods of building which seem to me almost impossible to use on small scale models.

Those making the simplified model may, of course, adopt any of the following details that they wish.

Cabin deck-house

This may be built up, instead of being a solid block, any semi-hard wood is good for this purpose; pear is perhaps the best but is hard to find, bass or poplar will do; there are cigar boxes that look like cedar, but are made of a white-wood which I have found excellent for this type of work.

The sides and top should be not less than $\frac{1}{16}$ in. thick. The corners should by rights, be tenoned into heavy corner posts, but this is only a waste of labor, and they should not even be mitred, but butted, so that they can be firmly glued together, and made to join up square.

The openings for the doors and windows should be cut out before joining up. Above the windows bore four small holes, and in them thread small wires, say No. 26, sticking the points into the lower edge of the windows. These painted white are the protecting bars. Back of these glue a piece of gelatine such as a photo film, for the glass. On the outside glue rabbeted battens twice the length of the windows, with their inside edges level with the windows; in these slide shutters the same size as the windows, to protect them in bad weather. Note that the windows are longer than they are deep. (See Fig. XXIII.)

The doors can be panelled, by cutting down the panel with a $\frac{1}{16}$ in. chisel and scratching in moldings, or the same effect can be obtained by raising the door-frame, with a thin cardboard overlay. They can be made to

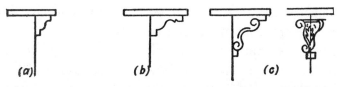

FIG. XLV.—Cabin-house moldings; a, at the sides, and abaft; b, at the forward edge; c, the brackets.

open, by hinging them, not with real hinges, which will be suggested by paper strips, or just painted on, but by driving a needle point up into the bottom and down into the top from the edge of the house, as close as possible to the back edge of the door; on these points it will swing.

When the doors and windows are made the four sides should be glued together. The top will be 1 ft. (real measurement) bigger than the sides, at the sides and after edge and 2 ft. at the forward edge. It can be glued on, then right round it on top glue a flat strip, 9 in. by 3 in. This is to prevent water running off the top onto the paint; at the corner there are scuppers, or holes to the under edge of the molding, with short spouts. With a

V gouge or small file make moldings of the projecting edges, and on either side of the cabin doors have a carved supporting bracket, extending about half-way down the house.

In Fig. XLV, a, is a side and astern molding; b, the forward molding and c, the side and front of the brackets.

Glue the house in position and right round it, at the deck level, glue a covering-board 1 ft. deep by 3 in. thick. This is to strengthen it and prevent leakage.

Forward Deck-house

The forecastle, or forward deck-house will be constructed in the same manner as the after one, except that the molding all the way round will be as the lighter one on that house. There will be a similar covering-board round on the top and at the bottom.

The doors and windows will be of the same construction, and in the positions shown in Fig. XXXIII. The galley doors should be in two halves, so that the top half can be opened to admit air while the lower half is closed to keep intruders out. This top half may be hinged and left open, as shown in the detail drawing, but should be back flat to the side of the house. If you like, the galley stove may be shown inside: it would be a block of wood about 3 ft. high, by the same width, extending ing right across, under the funnel.

On the fore end, in place of windows, there will be a rack for four capstan bars on either side. These racks are battens screwed horizontally, to the house. They are about 5 ft. long, 6 in. wide and 3 in. thick; in the top one are bored holes to take the thin end of the bars, and in the lower ones sockets to take the butt ends. (See detail in Fig. LIII.) Description of the capstan bars will be found under the Capstan sub-head.

None of the doors on this or the other house, come to the deck but to the top of the covering board only.

The dummy panels, between the doors, will be fashioned similarly to the doors, but with two panels, and nothing to open. They are just fancy-work to relieve the flat expanse of the house-side.

Boats and Skids

The boats and skids on the house will be the same as described for the simplified model, but the skids should have little staples on either side of each boat, and to these the boats should be lashed down.

On the skids, outside the boats should be lashed some light spare spars, or varying lengths, such as stu'ns'l booms.

The funnel will be the same, but may have four guys, (stays) to prevent it blowing away. They should be very thin.

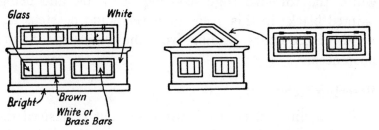

FIG. XLVI.—Skylight details. Scale 1/8".

Skylight

The skylight may be the same, but built up like the houses, with gelatine windows and bars, but no shutters. A ship of this class would, however, most probably, have a glass top to the skylight, it would then be as in Fig. XLVI. The gabled top being set on the flat skylight.

The two sides of the top should by rights be openable by hinges at their top edges.

Companion-way

This again will be the same as described before, but the slide should be more carefully made. Its construction will be seen in the detail drawing on this page. The top panel slides in grooved moldings, like those for the window shutters.

An interesting finish is obtained by having the slide partly or wholly back, and the doors open. If this is done the wood should be first cut away underneath, square with the cover at the sides and after end and painted white, the forward edge scooping out a bit and being painted black; in this opening there should be steps the width of the doors, leading from the main deck, to the poop deck.

Steering Gear

This again will be much the same, but if desired the legs of the cover-box may be on a framework, so that the cover itself can lift off, disclosing the drum with a rope round it; this rope will come up through the deck, round the drum and into the deck again; just stick the ends of the rope into glued holes in the deck. (Fig. XLVII.)

Across the deck, under the wheel there should be a grating, for the man-at-the-wheel to stand on, saving wear on the deck and keeping his feet dry. It would be 4 ft. wide, 10 ft. long and about 2½ in. thick. Such a grating would in reality have an edge about 4 in. wide, with 1½ in. cross-strips. It can be made of thin strips

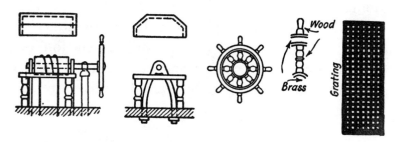

FIG. XLVII.—Steering-gear details. Scale 1/8″.

of wood half-lapped together, from the solid, or from a piece of celluloid. It would be bright.

Binnacle

This will be the same as for the model A, but the top panel may be shown open, disclosing a tiny compass inside.

Hatches

The hatch coamings (sides) were built of two substantial pieces with dove-tailed corners, but this is unnecessary in a model. If, however, you wish them to open, make the sides of strips of wood 1 ft. thick by 2 ft. high, with a rabbet on the inside top edge, to take the hatch covers, of which there should be three on each side, resting in the rabbets, and in a rabbet in a substantial bar across the center of the opening, fore-and-aft, which in turn rests in notches cut in the ends of the coamings. (See Fig. XLVIII.)

These hatches may have rings, lying in hollows, on two corners of each, to lift them by. If this plan is adopted then the decks should be cut through, inside the hatch coamings.

The hatches are covered at sea by three stout tarpaulins. In order to retain these firmly in position, on each side of the coaming, outside, there are cleats, say three to a side, the edges of the tarpaulins come to these; flat iron bars, are dropped in and wedged tight. If you put the tarpaulins on, it seems hardly necessary to con-

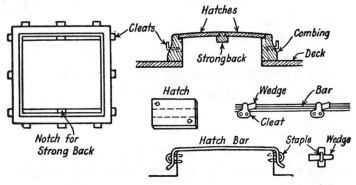

Fig. XLVIII.— Details for building a hatchway. Scale 1/8″.

struct the inside of the hatches, but in either case have the cleats.

U shaped, flat iron bars, similar in section to those at the sides are laid over the hatches, at the ends. When battened-down, the ends of these slip over staples in the coamings and are retained by round wedges.

The after hatch would have these wooden hatch covers, usually termed just "hatches" but as a rule would be covered with a "booby-hatch," to admit readily such passengers as may have been carried below and to make store rooms, etc., accessible. This, in construction, is like the companion-way. It sits on the after hatch, raising it by about 1½ ft. and is lashed to the deck by ring-bolts at each corner. (See Fig. XLIX.)

There should, most probably, also be a small hatch, say 4 ft. sq. between the forecastle head and the fore-ward fife-rail. It would be of similar construction to the main hatch.

Fife-rails

In the making of the fife-rails we cannot improve much on that already described, the rails at the main should,

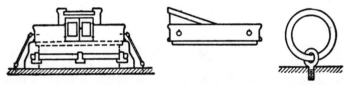

Fig. XLIX.—Booby-hatch details. Scale 1/8″. Ring-bolt.

however, be about ⅛ in. longer, to contain the pump gear, and support the flywheels, and should have two stanchions, one at the extreme end and the other, ⅜ in. forward of that.

Pumps

The pumps were omitted altogether in the model A, but if you can make a neat job of them, they should be included. They would be of the plunger, crank, flywheel type, and may be seen in Fig. L. First make the crank from a piece of wire, bending it sharply at the angles, having the axle straight, and leaving enough at the ends to bend up, and down, for the handles. For the plungers take two short lengths of wire, flatten the ends, and bend them round the cranks; lay the crank across the fife-rail and mark where the ends of the plungers come, (they should divide the space between the rails into three equal parts.) With these marks as centers, drive into the deck two short lengths of brass pipe of about 1 ft. dia. representing the pump wells. Pieces of tin or brass, bent round will do, or celluloid, or even lead. If tapping them into place gives them a slightly turned rim, so much the better.

Two flywheels of 5 ft. dia. are wanted. You may be able to find rings of the right diameter, if not brass wire

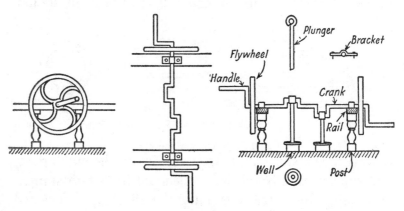

FIG. L.—Pumps.

bent round and soldered may be used, to these are soldered the spokes, of the shape indicated, which are flattened where they cross, a hole is bored at the cross and they are forced onto the crank wire, outside the rails. The wires are then bent as close as possible to the wheels, to form the handles. The cranks are then fastened to the fife-rail with bearings of thin strips of metal, nailed with pin heads, or with pin staples, so that the ends of the plungers are in the wells. All this will be black or dark green, except the spokes which should be scarlet.

If not handy at small soldering, the flywheels can be made in one piece from celluloid or lead.

Bitt-heads

The bitts will be the same as previously described, but, if the scale is large enough, they should be rounded to represent wear, where it would come. This applies also to the posts of the fife-rails, the forward parts of which may have projecting bolsters, similar to the bitts.

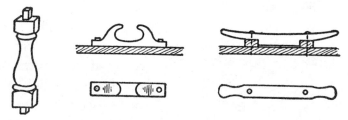

FIG. LI.—Stanchion and cleats.

Bulwark Cleats, or Cavels

As well as the bitts there should be cleats on the bulwarks for making fast heavy ropes, such as light mooring ropes, and the fore and main sheets.

Fig. LI gives the construction of these. They may be of wood or celluloid, and be fastened with pin points as well as glue, and painted white. They should fit right back to the bulwark, and be notched over the stanchions. There would be one on either side under the main and under the fore shrouds.

Chocks

To guide the mooring ropes, there should be chocks on the rail at each bow and on the round of the quarters. Their shape is shown in Fig. LI. Those at the stern were usually on the rail, and at the bow let into it, in which case it will be sufficient to cut notches of that shape. About halfway between the stem and the cathead will be the right position for the forward ones.

Ladders

For the ladders there is nothing to add, unless your

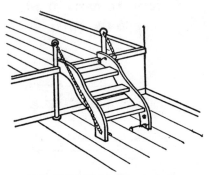

FIG. LII.—Monkey-poop ladder.

scale will permit of much more elaborate work. If so they should be as shown in Fig. LII. The sides are gracefully curved. They have hooks, and staples or small lashings through rings on either side, top and bottom, to retain them, and they have canvas covered ropes, with fancy knots, to hold to, when ascending, these come from a short stanchion at top to a seizing at the lower step.

It should be remembered that the sides and steps were only $1\frac{1}{2}$ in. thick by about 10 in. wide, so you cannot make them too light. If made of brass or tin, that would be better.

Capstan

Our capstan, if the scale permits, may be a much more careful construction, as seen in Fig. LIII. It is a solid iron stationary base, with a pawl-rim, or ring of notches. The capstan proper is on a stout shank which goes through the base to a plate in the main deck; the middle is curved so that the rope round it slips to its centre;

the flat rim above had usually six square holes to take the butts of the capstan-bars, and the lower edge had six or eight pawls, which engaged the notches of the pawl-rim, thus preventing it from slipping back. The top was more or less dome shaped, and called the "drumhead." It stood about 4 ft. high, by 3 ft. dia. at the base, and 2 ft. dia. at the top. Several types were in use at this time, that marked a, being the most likely one for this ship.

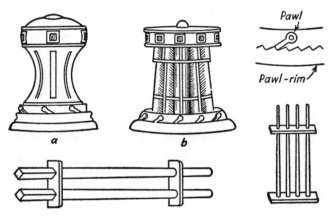

Fig. LIII.—Two kinds of capstans and capstan-bars.

Capstan-bars

These are the wooden bars, which were shipped in the holes in the capstan when a rope was to be hove in. Their butts were put into the holes, then men pushed on them, walking round the capstan. They were about 7 ft. long, by 4 in. sq. at the butts, rounding quickly and tapering to about 2½ in. at the ends. They were of ash and kept scraped bright. They stood in the racks previously described, on the end of the forecastle-house. Others were sometimes housed horizontally in racks inside the rail on the fore part of the forecastlehead, two and two.

Bells

The bells will be the same, but the forward one may have a finer bracket. Some were hung from one bracket, which was just a curved iron post bolted to the deck, but the more elaborate ones were hung in brackets of dolphins, tail up. The illustration, Fig. LIV shows a pair that were recently sold by auction and are quite typical. They should be painted a green bronze.

FIG. LIV.—Two methods of supporting the forward bell.

After Boats

There is nothing to add to the after boats, but the correct form of davits is shown in Fig. LV. The ends of the boat falls make fast to the pin-cleats and should have some of the cord coiled on them. A light spar (5 in. dia. in the middle) should be lashed across them, with fenders in the middle, at a height to catch the gunwhale of the boat when it is lashed to them. The lashings should be flat ropes (sennet) with eyes at each end, the top eyes are seized to the davit heads, the lashings then come under the boat and with light ropes bouse tight to rings in the bulwark, thus when at sea preventing the boat from swinging about. The l o w e r ends of the guys should h a v e two single blocks a n d falls, the lower blocks being hooked to rings in the bulwark, or may have thimbles and lanyards as seen at the right hand guy.

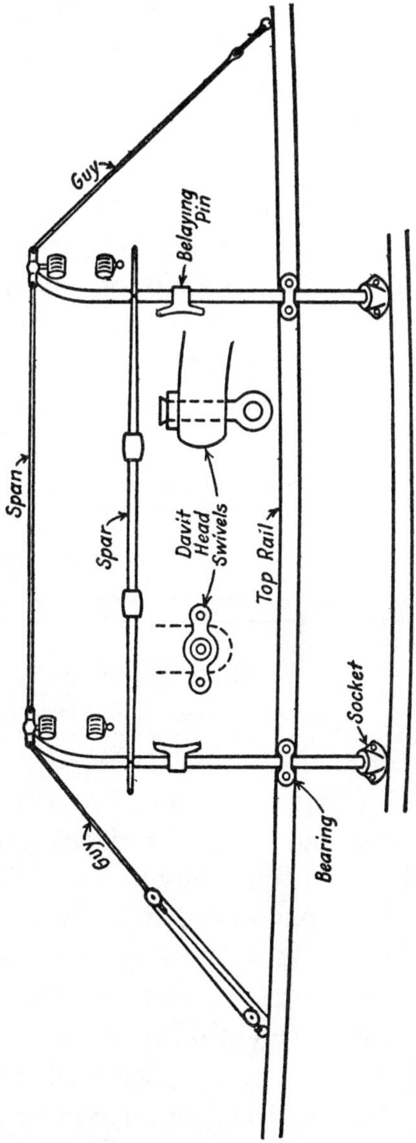

Taffrail

The only difference to be made in the taffrail is to use turned wooden posts, if you can, but they are very difficult to make, and the ends to set in the rail above and below are very liable to break off. If you make them, paint the square parts (Fig. LI) white and have the rest bright.

Spare spars

On either side of the deck close to the

Fig. LV.—Davits and boat-spar.

waterways, there should be a spare spar, for use in case of accident. One should be of the size of a topmast and the other of a top-gallant yard, but they should be octagonal, instead of being round. They sit in chocks, and are lashed with chains to bolts in the waterways. They would be painted white.

Ring-bolts

These are stout iron rings of about 6 in. dia. fastened to the deck by an eye bolt, with a plate and nut underneath. There should be one at each corner of the hatches, others in the waterway, for the spare spars to lash to, and one on each side of the forecastlehead for temporary anchor-fluke lashings.

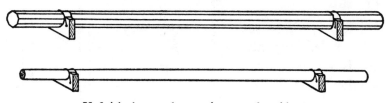

Unfinished spars for use in case of accident.

Fig. LVI.—Topmast.   Fig. LVII.—Top-gallant-yard.

It is said to be unlucky to stub the right toe on one of these but lucky to stub the left—it hurts equally with either, and frequently happens, therefore do not put them too far from the hatches, say about $1\frac{1}{2}$ ft.

To make a number of rings of the same size, I screw up a stiff wire or thick needle in the vice, then wind some suitable wire (in this case No. 24 brass) round it, making a little spring, then with sharp nippers I cut this lengthwise, bringing the two ends of each piece together with pliers or a tap with a hammer. As they do not have to stand any real strain they need not be soldered. Suitable rings may sometimes be found in fishing tackle stores. These are fastened to the deck with bent-pin staples. Others will be required on each corner of the booby-hatch.

Cargo Winch

Close up to the after edge of the main hatch, there should be a winch, with which to hoist out the cargo.

Fig. LVIII shows this instrument of torture (especially on a hot day). It has a large and a small wooden barrel, each about 6 ft. long, with cogs at each end, these are supported on an iron frame bolted to the deck; the ends of the shaft of the upper, and smaller one, are squared to take handles. Two or four men get on these

Fig. LVIII.—Cargo winch.

handles and turn them, winding the rope on the small drum, for light weights, but for heavy lifts it moves over until its cogs engage those of the lower drum, thus giving much more purchase to a rope on that drum. There are pawls from the top bar to the upper cogs.

Water Butt

On the main deck, at the corner formed by the forecastle-head of the bulwark, there may stand a large water-butt (cask). In this the daily supply of fresh water was kept. It was free to all when water was plentiful but kept locked up when it was scarce.

As previously mentioned any of the fittings given in this chapter may be made for the simplified model, but as many fine details are also omitted from the rigging they seem to me hardly necessary or in keeping.

If they are made, great care be exercised to ensure their being neat and to scale, because it is, of course, better to have a good simple fitting rather than a clumsy one with elaborate details.

FRESHENING BREEZE

DECK VIEW.

"THE SOVEREIGN OF THE SEAS."
From a contemporary lithograph.

CHAPTER VI

MAKING THE SPARS, ETC.

BEFORE starting to make the spars please turn back to the first chapter and read the remarks about having them as near as possible to scale.

Some model makers cut their spars (masts, yards, booms, etc.) from straight grained white pine, but I prefer to use dowel sticks, which are stronger, of good color and can be bought nearly to size. They are sold a full $\frac{1}{4}''$, $\frac{3}{16}''$ and $\frac{1}{8}''$ dia. Use only straight grained ones, that will plane smoothly on all sides. For bringing them down to the right diameters I have found holding them on a flat board and planing them the easiest method, finishing them up with a scraper and sandpaper doubled in the palm of the hand. I work on one end of the whole stick, so as to have something to hold firmly. For the yards I plane from the center thus; cut them off to the right length, then holding the plane face-up between my knees or in the vice, shave down the other end, always leaving plenty for the scraping and sandpapering processes.

Their lengths and thicknesses will be found on the large RIGGING PLAN. For the length, if working to the same scale, you may lay the stick on the plan and cut off by that.

For the benefit of those working to other scales the measurements are given in feet and inches. Thus if a spar is marked as 48 ft. long, and one is working to a

$\frac{1}{8}$th scale that would be 48, $\frac{1}{8}$ths or 6 in. or if 15 in. dia. then it would be $\frac{5}{32}$ in. on the model.

It will be noticed that each mast tapers but slightly. The lower masts and bowsprit taper the most, being about $\frac{1}{3}$ rd. less at the top than the bottom. The heel of the topmast is but a shade less than the head of the lowermast, and the taper is only about $\frac{1}{16}$th, because the parral of the yard has to slide up and down it. The topgallant, royal and skysail masts, in one piece, do not individually taper at all, but there is a dip or shoulder, called the "stop," at the head of each, making the mast, as a whole, reduce about $\frac{3}{5}$ths from the heel to the head, and from there on (the pole) it tapers rapidly.

The yards taper from the slings (middle) to the yard-arms (ends) but not in a straight line nor an even curve. The proportional dimensions of a real yard is given so that you may get the idea right, but, of course one cannot work to so minute a scale. Each side of the yard is divided into four quarters, at the first the yard is $\frac{30}{31}$ of the center measurement, at the second $\frac{7}{8}$ at the third $\frac{7}{10}$ and at the end $\frac{3}{7}$, or $\frac{1}{2}$, with a stop, of about 1 in., where the brace band fits. This is shown graphically in Fig. LIX.

Lower-masts

On the lower-mast, mark from the head to the deck-line, beyond this, if the hull is solid, leave about $\frac{3}{4}$ in. to go in the deck, but if hollow, then enough to extend to the bottom, and at the lower end of it sink the head of a short nail, with the point extending to act as a mast-step. Mark also the under edge of the tops, which are platforms to spread the top-mast rigging. Cut a slight flat place on either side of the masts, to this mark, to take the cheeks seen in Fig. LX. They should be less than $\frac{1}{16}$ in.

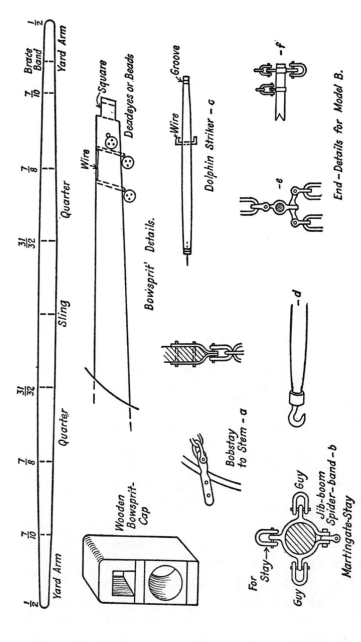

Yard Arm — ½ — 7/10 — 7/8 — 31/32 — Sling — 31/32 — 7/8 — 7/10 — Brace Band — ½ — Yard Arm

Quarter — Quarter — Quarter

Square

Wire

Deadeyes or Beads

Bowsprit' Details.

Wooden Bowsprit-Cap

Bobstay to Stem - a

For Stay

Guy — Guy

Jib-boom Spider-band - b

Martingate-Stay

-d

Groove

Wire

Dolphin Striker - c

-e

-f

End - Details for Model B.

Fig. LIX.—Tapering a yard. Fittings for the bowsprit. Dolphin-striker, with its lower end irons, e,f, and upper end hook, d. A wooden bowsprit cap, bobstay-plate, to fasten the bobstay. Jib-boom spider-band, b.

thick and made of hard or semi-hard wood, glue them in place making sure that they lie parallel, and aid the glue with a bank-pin driven through and clinched. Cut the masthead square with two sides in line with the cheeks.

For model A. Bore a $\frac{1}{16}$ in. hole through the mast, athwart, $\frac{11}{16}$ in. below the top, and another of the same size fore-and-aft $\frac{3}{16}$ in. below that—the first for the futtock shrouds and the latter for the yard trusses. The

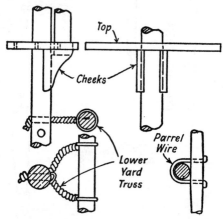

Fɪɢ. LX.—Cheeks of the lower-masts. Lower-yard trusses, and parral for other yards.

distances should be $\frac{1}{16}$ in. less at the fore and $\frac{3}{16}$ in. less at the mizzen (after) mast. In the fore and main-masts the head of a small nail or stout pin should be driven in, on the fore side, $\frac{5}{8}$ in. from the deck-mark, and at the main there should be a wire band with an eye abaft, $1\frac{1}{2}$ in. below the top, for the mizzen braces.

These holes will not be required for model B. Note: Before making any parts for the finer model, look through Chapter VIII for the additional instructions.

The lower-mast will be painted white.

Top-masts

The top-masts will be squared on both ends, sufficient to go through the tops and caps. Mark the station of the under sides of the cross-trees, bore a small hole athwart and through it push a pin or needle point, extending about $\frac{1}{8}$ in. on either side, to support the cross-trees, $\frac{1}{4}$ in. below this mark bore a $\frac{1}{16}$ in. hole athwart, for the top-gallant rigging, and just above that a small hole for the topsail-yard-halliards.

The topmasts are white where they double with the masts above and varnished or stain-varnished between.

Top-gallant, Royal, Skysail-masts

These three masts in one, must be carefully made. The plane will only bring them down to the general line; the shoulders must then be cut, each being only very slight, and the lengths between scraped to even thicknesses. The heel will be squared to fit the cross-trees. At $\frac{1}{8}$ in. below each stop, bore a small hole fore-and-aft for the respective halliards. Get three flat beads about $\frac{3}{32}$ in. dia. and fit these to the ends for trucks, but do not glue them on yet.

Globular trucks are really more correct for American ships, but the flat ones look better.

These masts will be white at the doublings and mastheads and bright between.

Bowsprit

The bowsprit will be a full $\frac{3}{16}$ in. at the heel, tapering to about $\frac{1}{4}$ less at the end. The end will be squared, as was the lower-mast-head. At $\frac{3}{16}$ in. from the end bore a small hole athwart; through this pass a very thin wire, twisting a bead or deadeye to each end, so that they lie close up to the spar. At $\frac{1}{4}$ in. and $\frac{7}{16}$ in. from the end bore holes vertically through the bowsprit and similarly fasten a bead to each end of a wire passed through both holes. (See Fig. LIX.)

This will be white.

Jib-boom

The jib-boom tapers slightly to the first collar (stop) then runs straight to the next, and from there tapers again, the extreme end being rather less than half the thickness of the heel. The heel is cut on a bevel to lie snug against the forecastle rail; there is a small vertical hole at the inner stop and three holes in line, close to each other at the outer stop. This may be seen in the rigging plan and profile.

It is white at the stop and end, and bright elsewhere.

These and other holes bored to take ropes will, naturally, be of such size that the rope can just be passed through, and must be kept down as small as possible.

Martingale-boom or Dolphin-striker

This is the short spar under the end of the bowsprit, which acts on the cantilever principle, to keep the end of the jib-boom down, and must consequently be comparatively strong. It is one inch long by a bare $\frac{3}{32}$ in. dia. in the center, tapering at both ends. The top end is bored for a headless pin, the point of which projects into a hole in the lower edge of the cap, and slightly into the bowsprit. At $\frac{5}{8}$ in. from the top bore a hole through it, push a short piece of copper wire through and bend the ends down. (See Fig. LIX.) At $\frac{1}{8}$ in. from the lower end do the same and just under that put a fine wire or thread binding, to prevent it splitting; this may well be done at the top end also.

It is better to make this piece out of stout brass or copper wire, but that is a lot more trouble.

This will be painted white.

Trysail-mast

This mast, which cannot be shown very clearly on the rigging plan, is for the hoops of the spanker to run on. It will be a bare $\frac{1}{8}$ in. dia. throughout; it stands about $\frac{1}{16}$ in. abaft the mizzen-lower-mast; sets in a hole in the cabin-top, and has a small hole in the other end to take a pin point through the mizzen-top.

It will be stain-varnished.

Spanker-boom

This spar tapers about $\frac{1}{3}$rd to the mast and $\frac{1}{2}$ to the end, the thickest part being one third the distance from the mast. It should have an athwartship hole $\frac{1}{4}$ in. from the end, and at the heel it should have a wire eye to fit tightly round the mast, with a point going into the boom end.

It will be painted white.

Gaff

The spanker-gaff will be of the same shape but more slender. It has an athwart hole $\frac{1}{4}$ in. from the outer end, for the vangs, a very small wire eye at the extreme end for the flag-halliards and a wire eye at the heel to slide on the trysail-mast.

This will be white.

Yards

The shape of yards was described on page 86 and the lengths and diameters will be found on the rigging plan. Note that each in succession is a shade smaller than the one before, in the order of main, fore and mizzen and from down-up.

The yards of these ships were sometimes bright; with white or black yard-arms; painted all black or all white. The last mentioned was I believe the style for "The Sovereign of the Seas."

Lower-yards

The fore, main and cross-jack (pronounced crojack) yards were supported in the middle by fixed trusses or cranse-irons of various construction, similar to those now in use. The usual form is a U shaped iron arm bolted to bands on the yard, which pivots on another band round the mast, as shown in Fig. LXVII.

As the yards in our simplified model will not have to swing round we can make the truss in one piece, and the easiest way to get the right shape is to bend a piece of soft copper wire in the shape of the U, then tightly round the yard $\frac{1}{4}$ in. on each side of the center, twisting the ends back round the U part and then together, this latter part to go through the hole we made in the mast. (See Fig. LX). When this piece is thickly coated with paint it will look like one piece.

At $\frac{3}{8}$ in. from the ends bore small vertical holes in the yards.

Topsail and top-gallant-yards.

These yards will have parrals instead of trusses, because they should slide up and down the masts. To simulate these bore holes in the yards in the middle, the thickness of the mast apart, through these put a loop of copper wire, just large enough for the mast to slide in and clinch the ends down on the fore side of the yards. (See Fig. LX.)

Bore vertical holes for the lifts at the positions shown, and in the middle for the ends of the halliards.

Royal and Skysail-yards

These yards will be the same, except that they are too small to have the vertical holes.

Tops

These and the following pieces may be made of wood or metal, but celluloid makes the easiest and most satisfactory job. If it is white then it will not need painting. It should be about $\frac{1}{16}$ in. thick, or thicker for the caps.

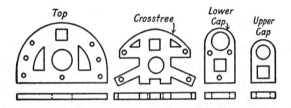

Fig. LXI.—Simple tops, crosstrees and caps.

The round holes in the tops should be bored first, to fit snugly over the lower-mast-heads, the square holes to take the heels of the topmasts should be just in the position shown in Fig. LXI. At either side are the lubber-holes through which the rigging passes and at the outer rim three holes for the futtock-shrouds, with one behind for topmast stays.

Top-mast-Cross-trees

These pieces represent four wooden parts, the trestle-trees, fore-and-aft and the cross-trees, athwart, with a bent piece across the fore side.

[93]

They fit over the topmast heads, in a similar manner to the tops.

Caps

These go at the lower and top-mast-heads. The thing to be careful about in making them is that the holes are so placed that when in position the masts will stand truly parallel, with the upper dead in front of the lower. The space between its masts being about one-half the thickness of the masts.

The sizes given in Fig. LXI are for the fore and main, for the mizzen the parts should be about $\frac{1}{5}$th smaller.

Bowsprit-cap

This will be the same as a lower-mast cap, except that the round and square holes should be bored at an angle so that it will sit almost vertical. It will not need the holes through the face of it, but should have a small one through the lower edge to take the spike of the martingale.

Block Making

In model A, we are going to eliminate quite a number of the blocks (pulleys) but cannot do so entirely and still have a good model, therefore there will be needed, 48 large single, 6 large double, 15 small single and 13 small double blocks.

Box-wood is the best for making these, but it is sometimes hard to find, unless one has an old two-foot rule or scale. Holly-wood or gum-wood serve the purpose almost equally well and the occasional splitting of one is more than compensated by the ease in cutting and boring.

Fig. XLII shows the construction of a real block and how they should be made for our purpose, the idea being to get as near the appearance of the real block, on as small a scale as possible. The large blocks mentioned will run from about 15 in. for the topsail-halliards or braces to 10 in. for the top-gallant-halliards or top-sail braces. The small blocks would be 7 or 8 in. in length, but one cannot make them thus small, so make the lesser ones as small as you can, to take the cord to be used for the running-gear, and the larger ones about half as big again. A double block will be thicker than a single but should be no longer.

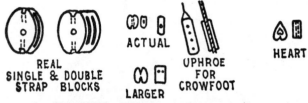

REAL
SINGLE & DOUBLE STRAP BLOCKS

ACTUAL

LARGER

UPHROE FOR CROWFOOT

HEART

FIG. LXII.—Blocks, uphroes and hearts.

The best way to make them is to plane up a strip to the right dimensions, then bore along it at the right distances, lay it with the holes horizontal and cut a slight groove down the middle, lay it flat with the holes vertical and nick it between the holes with a knife on both sides, turn it again and cut it in sections, then with a very small three-cornered file, round the ends, and continue the V grooves, over the ends, deepest at the corners.

If made of holly, you will have creamy-white blocks which look good, if of other wood they may be left bright, or painted white; this should be done before they are used.

That concludes the making of the spars and fittings

for the rigging for model A. For model B the spars, blocks and all measurements will be the same, but more elaborate fittings may be used; these will be described in Chapter VIII.

FRESH HEAD WIND

CHAPTER VII

THE RIGGING

Bowsprit

SHIP the bowsprit in its hole in the bow, with a touch of glue to steady it, and be very careful that it is truly in line with the keel.

Set up the bobstays, hooking the ends of two pieces of the heaviest chain, (which should have about 12 links to the inch) to staples driven into the stem, just above the water line; to the other ends, with thread or wire, fasten deadeyes or beads to come within about $\frac{1}{4}$ in. of those under the bowsprit. (Fig. LIX.) Reeve a thread for a lanyard, through the upper and lower eyes three times; draw the chains tight.

Drive wire eyes into the hull on both sides, under the main-deck molding and just abaft the catheads; to these hook smaller chains and tighten them to the beads or deadeyes at the sides of the bowsprit. These are the bowsprit-shrouds and should be well tight.

Lower-masts

The correct order for rigging the masts is fore, main and mizzen, but on a model it goes easier to rig the middle one first. The procedure will be the same for all three, therefore only the rigging of one will be described.

Step the mast and put the top in position. Bore holes in the ship's sides $\frac{1}{4}$ in. below the lower channels in line with the holes or grooves in them, as shown on the rigging plan. Take some of the heaviest cord, reeve one end through the holes in both channels, put a spot of glue on the end of the cord and the end of a toothpick broken in two and with this latter force the end of the

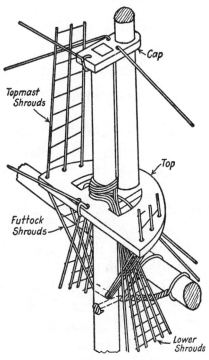

Fig. LXIII.—Perspective of a lowermast-head, showing the method of passing the rigging round the mast-head and the topmast rigging through the top and the mast.

cord in the hole and tap home, this will secure the end. Take the other end of the cord up through the lubber-hole in the top; round the mast from forward-aft; down through the top again; through the holes in the channels and fasten off as before, so that it will be well tight when the mast is dead upright, but raking aft the required amount. It is a good plan, with the shrouds, to rake the mast a little too much so that pulling them forward again with the stays will tighten them up still further.

The correct angle of the masts from the vertical, or rake, is $\frac{3}{4}$, $\frac{7}{8}$, and $1\frac{1}{8}$ in. to the foot, for the fore, main and mizzen, respectively. This makes them actually slightly fanwise, but gives them the appearance of being parallel.

The starboard, forward pair go on first, then the port, the second starboard, and so on, until at the fore and main there are three pairs to a side and at the mizzen two pair. Rack each pair together, close under the top.

The stays come next. The main-stay starts by being hitched or seized to a staple in the deck just forward of the foremast, the end reeves up through the lubber hole, round abaft the mast and down the other side, being hauled well tight and fastened off to a corresponding eye or staple.

The fore-stay sets up similarly to eyes in the deck, right forward. The mizzen stay comes down to the nail head in the foreside of the mainmast, near the deck, under which it is tightly tied with a neat reef knot. (Fig. LXIII.)

Ratlines

It is wise to "rattle down" or put the ratlines on as one proceeds, partly because it is a tedious job, best done in small spells, and partly because the less other gear there is in the way the better.

For this I use Nos. 24 to 30 black sewing cotton. I take a foot or so on a needle, clove-hitch it to the left hand shroud, then take it in and out the others and clove-hitch to the right hand shroud, at about $\frac{3}{16}$ in. intervals.

A ratline on a real ship has an eye-splice in each end, one is seized to the shroud, the ratline is then clove-hitched to the middle shrouds and seized to the last one, but this is too much work and would not look neat when done, thus the suggested plan is the better. Even this is rather much for our simplified model, and I would suggest threading the ratline through the outside shroud, in and out the others and through the last one.

In either case, at the fore and main, only every fifth ratline should come to the forward shroud, the others

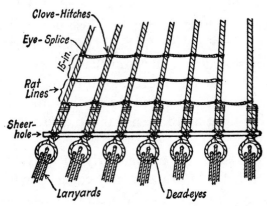

Showing the ratlines (steps) and sheerpole on a real vessel.

starting at the second shroud. They should be evenly spaced, and tight across but not so as to draw the shrouds together. Do not cut them off very close while working. When they are all on, give the whole a coat of thin, black shellac, when this is dry cut the ends off close to the shrouds with fine scissors or a splinter of razor blade. The latter is best, but be careful not to cut the shrouds also.

The lower-yards may be swayed aloft now, but I prefer to leave them until later.

Top-masts

Ship the lower cap on the head of the lower-mast, through it reeve the top-mast, setting the heel into the square hole in the top, slip the top-sail-yard on, then put the cross-trees in position.

Set up the top-mast rigging. This can be all in one piece of the medium thickness cord. Start by passing it

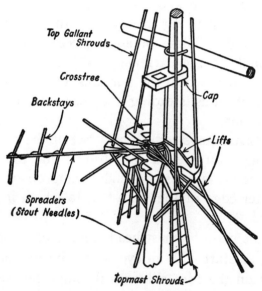

Fig. LXIV.—Perspective of the topmast-crosstrees, showing the passing of the rigging over the mast head, the topgallant-shrouds and backstay spreaders.

up through one of the holes in the edge of the top; up through the cross-trees; round the mast; down again; through the next hole in the top, on the same side; through the athwart hole in the mast; up through a hole in the other side of the top, and so on until you have three on each side, then the two ends can be knotted together, under the top. This will give the topmast rigging and futtock shrouds (underneath the top) all in one piece. This should have ratlines from where the futtock shrouds meet the lower shrouds to the mast head.

Next come the topmast-backstays. They start, as with the shrouds, from a hole in the hull, through the channels, between the arms of the cross-trees, round the mast and down again, giving one pair on each side. Be careful not to pull the mast to one side with these.

To prevent these and the masts above being set up awry, it is safest to rig them first with temporary back stays and stays. These would be pieces of cord hitched at the middle to the extreme mast-head, the backstays being brought down to the bumkins and the stay round the bowsprit, thus steading the masts firmly in their right positions.

The topmast-stays come next. Set up the mizzen first starting with an eye passing behind the topmast and through the cross-trees, the end coming down to a hole in the after edge of the main-top, to which it is seized or hitched.

From the main-topmast-head there is also a preventer backstay, so start with an eye round the foremast to the nail cleat on the fore side; up through the cross-trees; behind the mast; down the other side and to a hole in the fore-cap, racking the two together close under the fore-side of the cross-trees.

Jib-boom

The jib-boom will now have to be shipped and stayed. Put the bowsprit-cap in position, reeve the jib-boom through it and pass the gammoning lashing round the two about $\frac{1}{4}$ in. from the heel of the latter, with a cross turn or two between, keeping them slightly apart and tightening the lashing. This gammoning was in later days of chain, wedged tight.

Put the dolphin-striker in position. Lash a piece of the small chain to the boom end at the outer collar or stop, bring it down to the end of the dolphin-striker, lash it there, so that it will be tight when the spar is almost vertical; take it back and lash it to the boom again at the first stop. The lashings may be fine sewing thread. Now lash the bight of a similar piece of chain to the same place on the dolphin-striker but abaft; bring the ends back, one on either side and bowse them well tight to the ends of the catheads, with a piece of thin wire, or beads or deadeyes, as with the bowsprit shrouds. Gently hang a weight on the end of the jib-boom when doing this, so as to get them very tight, and be sure that the strain is even on both sides.

Hitch the bight of a piece of the heavy cord to the boom at the first stop; bring the ends down to the inner holes in the catheads, draw them tight and fasten off with a toothpick peg. Do the same from the end stop, with medium cord to the middle hole in the catheads.

Fore-topmast-stays

Two stays come from the fore-topmast. Start with an eye round the bowsprit and jib-boom, up through the cross-trees, as at the main, and then down through the hole at the first stop; under the hook on the dolphin-striker and back to an eye in the hull under the cathead. Rack the two parts together as at the main.

Topsail-yards

As neat a way as any for the lifts for this model is to pass the end of a piece of the heavy cord through the yard, with a knot underneath; then through the cross-trees, between the masts and to the other yard arm, finishing off with a small knot again; a touch of glue in the middle of the cord will be sufficient to hold the yard horizontal when hanging in the lifts.

The neatest way to make these knots is to open the cord and knot the two parts together with a touch of glue, cutting the ends off close.

The halliards may start in the same way with a knot under the yard in the middle; then through the hole in the mast-head. Fasten a large single block to the other end of this to lie fairly close up when the yard is down; through this reeve another heavy cord, hitch or seize one end to the top and to the other seize a large double block; to a staple in the deck fasten another double (or single) block; reeve a piece of the lightest cord through these and fasten off with a peg to the bulwark when all is tight and the yard right down in the lifts. The tackle at the fore comes to the port side, abreast the topmast backstays, at the main to starboard and at the mizzen to port again. The braces will be left until later.

Top-gallant-masts

Ship the topmast-cap and top-gallant-mast as described for the topmasts. Ship the top-gallant yard. Seize or hitch the stay, of the medium cord to the stop at the mast-head; set up the top-gallant rigging as for the topmast, except that the cord will go up to the mast-head and back down on the same side, with an eye seized in the bight; set up the backstays, one on either side, seized at the top, and then set up the stays. The mizzen-top-gallant-stay comes down to a hole abaft the main cap; the main comes to a hole in the fore-cross-trees and the fore through a hole at the second stop in the jib-boom then under the hook in the dolphin-striker, on the side opposite

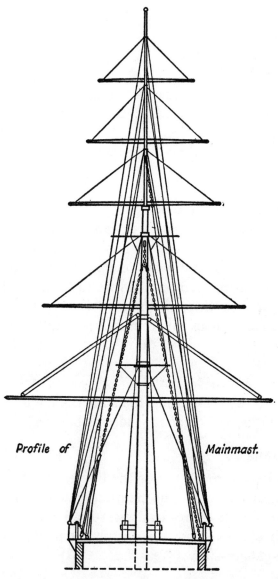

Profile of   Mainmast.

FIG. LXV.—Profile view of the mainmast, showing, in particular, the spread of the rigging, and the lead of the halliards.

[105]

to the topmast-stay (inner-jib-stay) and thence to the ship's side.

Top-gallant-yard

This is rigged the same as the topsail-yard, but with a lighter cord. The halliards come right down, with a double and a single block, to a staple in the deck, on the opposite side of the deck to the topsail-halliards.

Royal-masts

These being of the same spars as the top-gallant-masts will be already in position. Put the yards on. Seize the eyes of the stays at the stops and bring down a backstay on either side. The stay at the mizzen comes to the main cross-trees, at the main to the fore-top-gallant-mast-head and at the fore through the next hole in the jib-boom, under the same hook and to the same staple as the inner-jib-stay.

Royal-yards

As with the top-gallant, the halliards having only two single blocks, and reversing sides as before.

Skysail-masts

As with the royal, but of the lightest cord. The stay at the mizzen comes to the main-top-gallant-mast-head, at the main to the fore-royal-mast-head and at the fore through the outer hole in the jib-boom, then following the top-gallant-stay.

Skysail-yards

As the royal, except that they are rather fine for boring therefore the lifts should be hitched or seized round the yard-arms enough end being left to form the braces and the halliards can come straight down to the rail without purchase, or with a whip only.

Lower-yards

The fore, main and crossjack (crojak-mizzen) yards must now be sent aloft. Press the long point of the parral through the hole in the mast and clinch it close behind, reeve the lifts through the holes in the yard-arms and the holes in either side of the caps, the ends of the lifts may, after knotting, extend for brace pennants if these are not to be of chain.

Outriggers

The uppermost backstays should have spreaders or outriggers, to give them more staying power on the masts. These can be needles. Take stout, No. 3 needles, slide the points along the upper side of the cross-trees, under the bights of the rigging and point them into the top-gallant-mast, so that they will extend horizontally at an angle with the keel of about 45 degrees. With a piece of thin thread, stretch the sky-sail backstay to the eye, and seize the royal and top-gallant backstays at even spaces between that and the cross-trees, outside the outrigger. (See Fig. LXIV.) For the mizzen, No. 4 needles will be long enough. Paint these white.

Braces

The braces are the cords by which the yards are swung round with the parrals as axis.

It will be found easiest to start at the top and work down. Beginning with the mizzen-skysail-braces; hitch them to the yard-arms or have them continuous with the lifts, reeve them through single blocks lashed to either side of the main-top-mast-cap and from thence through

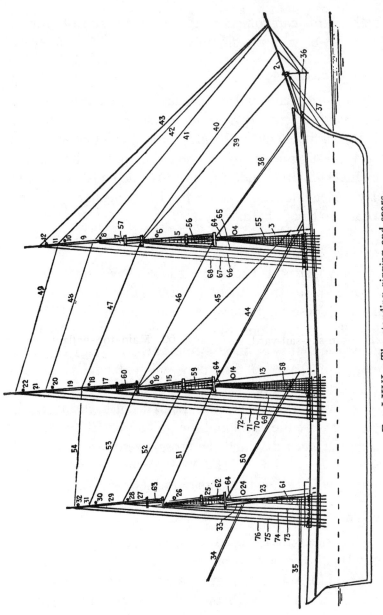

FIG. LXVI.—The standing rigging and spars.

THE STANDING RIGGING AND SPARS OF THE SOVEREIGN OF THE SEAS

The Spars
1. Bowsprit.
2. Jib-boom.
3. Fore-lower-mast.
4. Fore-yard.
5. Fore-top-mast.
6. Fore-top-sail-yard.
7. Fore-top-gallant-mast.
8. Fore-top-gallant-yard.
9. Fore-royal-mast.
10. Fore-royal-yard.
11. Fore-sky-sail-mast.
12. Fore-sky-sail-yard.
13. Main-mast.
14. Main-yard.
15. Main-top-mast.
16. Main-top-sail-yard.
17. Main-top-gallant mast.
18. Main-top-gallant-yard.
19. Main-royal-mast.
20. Main-royal-yard.
21. Main-sky-sail-mast.
22. Main-sky-sail-yard.
23. Mizzen-mast.
24. Cross-jack-yard.
25. Mizzen-top-mast.
26. Mizzen-top-sail-yard.
27. Mizzen-top-gallant-mast.
28. Mizzen-top-gallant-yard.
29. Mizzen-royal-mast.
30. Mizzen-royal-yard.
31. Mizzen-sky-sail-mast.
32. Mizzen-sky-sail-yard.
33. Try-sail-mast.
34. Spanker (or driver) gaff.
35. Spanker-boom.
36. Martingale-boom, or Dolphin-striker.

Rigging
37. Bobstays.
38. Fore-stay.
39. Fore-top-mast-stay.
40. Inner (or standing) jib-stay.
41. Fore-top-gallant-stay or, Outer-jib-stay.
42. Fore-royal-stay, or Flying-jib-stay.
43. Fore-sky-sail-stay.
44. Main-stay.
45. Main-top-mast-preventer-stay.
46. Main-top-mast-stay.
47. Main-top-gallant-stay.
48. Main-royal-stay.
49. Main-sky-sail-stay.
50. Mizzen-stay.
51. Mizzen-top-mast-stay.
52. Mizzen-top-gallant-stay.
53. Mizzen-royal-stay.
54. Mizzen-sky-sail-stay.
55. Fore-shrouds.
56. Fore-top-mast-rigging.
57. Fore-top-gallant-rigging.
58. Main-shrouds.
59. Main-top-mast-rigging.
60. Main-top-gallant-rigging.
61. Mizzen-shrouds.
62. Mizzen-top-mast-rigging.
63. Mizzen - top - gallant-rigging.
64. Futtock - shrouds (fore, main and mizzen).
65. Fore-top-mast (standing) backstays.
66. Fore-top-gallant-backstay.
67. Fore-royal-backstay.
68. Fore-sky-sail-backstay.
69. Main-top-mast-backstays.
70. Main-top-gallant-backstay.
71. Main-royal-backstay.
72. Main-sky-sail-backstay.
73. Mizzen - top - mast - backstays.
74. Mizzen-top-gallant-back-stay.
75. Mizzen-royal-backstay.
76. Mizzen-sky-sail-backstay.

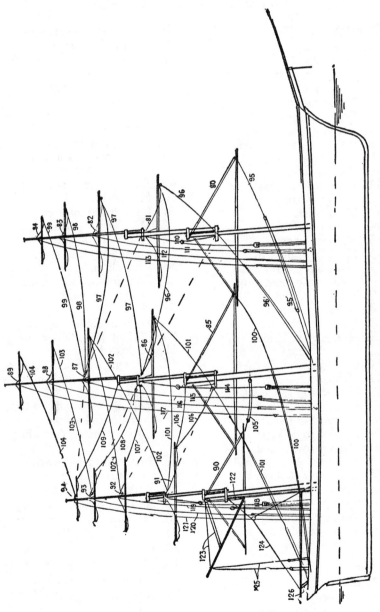

Fig. LXVII.—The running rigging. Braces must be fitted to both ends of the yards.

THE RUNNING RIGGING OF THE SOVEREIGN OF THE SEAS

80. Fore (topping) lifts.
81. Fore-top-sail-lifts.
82. Fore-top-gallant-lifts.
83. Fore-royal-lifts.
84. Fore-sky-sail-lifts.
85. Main-lifts.
86. Main-top-sail-lifts.
87. Main-top-gallant-lifts.
88. Main-royal-lifts.
89. Main-sky-sail-lifts.
90. Cross-jack-lifts.
91. Mizzen-top-sail-lifts.
92. Mizzen-top-gallant-lifts.
93. Mizzen-royal-lifts.
94. Mizzen-sky-sail-lifts.
95. Fore-braces.
96. Fore-top-sail-braces.
97. Fore-top-gallant-braces.
98. Fore-royal-braces.
99. Fore-sky-sail-braces.
100. Main-braces.
101. Main-top-sail-braces.
102. Main-top-gallant-braces.
103. Main-royal-braces.
104. Main-sky-sail-braces.
105. Cross-jack-braces.
106. Mizzen-top-sail-braces.
107. Mizzen - top - gallant - braces.
108. Mizzen-royal-braces.
109. Mizzen-sky-sail-braces.
110. Fore - top - sail - halliards (and tie).
111. Fore - top - gallant - halliards.
112. Fore-royal-halliards.
113. Fore-sky-sail-halliards.
114. Main-top-sail-halliards.
115. Main - top - gallant - halliards.
116. Main-royal-halliards.
117. Main-sky-sail-halliards.
118. Mizzen-top-sail-halliards.
119. Mizzen-top-gallant-halliards.
120. Mizzen-royal-halliards.
121. Mizzen-sky-sail-halliards.
122. Throat-halliards.
123. Peak-halliards.
124. Spanker-boom-topping-lifts.
125. Spanker - vang - pendants and falls.
126. Spanker-boom-sheet.

NOTE—Braces and halliards are shown curved for clearness. (Braces are shown on the weather (near) side only.)

the cross-trees to the deck, or as ours is only a simplified model, all the skysail and royal braces may be brought through the cross-trees and be tied underneath them.

The idea in leading all running gear, is to get them so that they are clear of the sails, and do not rub against each other, or the standing rigging. In a real ship this requires extra blocks and bulls-eye leads, but these we can dispense with.

The main-skysail-braces lead through a small double block lashed under the eye of the mizzen-skysail stay. The mizzen-royal-braces lead through a similar block lashed under the lower eye of the mizzen-royal stay. The main-royal-braces lead through a double block under the upper eye of the same stay. The mizzen-top-gallant-braces lead through single blocks lashed close up under the after side of the main-cross-trees. The main top-gallant braces start by being hitched to the eye of the mizzen-topmast-stay, then through blocks at the yard-arms and back through blocks lashed to the eye of the mizzen-top-gallant-stay, and down through the top to belaying-pins in the monkey-rail.

The mizzen-topsail-braces start with a hitch at the main-lower-cap, through blocks at the yard-arms, back through blocks lashed to the lower eye of the mizzen-top-mast-stay and down to the bulwark, under the rigging. The main-topsail-braces, start with a hitch at the same place as the top-gallant-braces, through blocks at the yard-arms and from there to blocks lashed to the monkey-rail, abaft the bumkins, belaying to pins forward of these. Before making these fast the cross-jack-braces had better be rove off. The cross-jack yard should have short pendants (which may be continuations of the lifts) with large single blocks at the ends. To the wire eye at the mainmast, under the top, are seized two double blocks.

The brace starts by being hitched to the heel of the pendant block, reeves through the double one, back through the first, through the double again and then down to the main-fife-rail, on either side.

For the main-braces there are pendants, about 2 in. long pegged to the end of the bumkin, or seized to eyes in them, with large single blocks at the other ends. From the yard-arms there should be other pendants, of small chain for preference, with single blocks at the ends. The fall starts from the heel of the upper block; through the lower; through the upper and down through a single block lashed to the rail, forward of the last ones.

The fore-sky-sail and royal-braces are lead through double blocks lashed on either side of the eye of the main-top-gallant-stay. The fore-top-gallant-braces start with a hitch just underneath these blocks, through blocks at the yard-arms, through blocks lashed close up under the main-cross-trees and down to the fife-rail. The fore-top-sail-braces start with a hitch at the eye of the main top-mast-stay, through blocks at the yard-arms and down to blocks lashed to the ends of the main-channels, making fast by being pegged to the bulwarks about an inch forward of the blocks. The fore-braces have pendants similar to those of the main and come to a block lashed to the bulwark just forward of the channels and are finished off similarly.

The braces should all be of the thinnest grade of cord, and should be tight, but not pulled so tight as to slack the stays. Make sure that the yards are down as far as the lifts and halliards will allow, before fastening them off.

Spanker-boom and gaff

These have been left until the last, because they are likely to get knocked whilst working at other gear. The lower end of the try-sail-mast should be shipped in its hole. Reeve the wire eyes of the boom and gaff on this, press it into position and drive a small nail or stout pin through the after edge of the top, into it. Give the eye of the boom a pinch with the pliers to keep it from sliding up and down; it should be about $\frac{1}{4}$ in. above the top of the cabin-house.

To the inner end of the gaff fasten a single block and another to the hole abaft the cap, through these reeve the throat halliards, bringing the end down to the rail. To the outer end hitch another line, reeve it through a double block fastened to the cap, then through a single block lashed to the gaff at about one third from the end, back through the double block and down to the rail on the opposite side. For the vangs hitch a line to the end and bring their ends to the rail, steadying the gaff amidships. From the same place bring a line down to the end of the boom, suspending it horizontally.

To the after edge of the top hitch a line about two inches long with a single block at each end. From the end of the boom bring lines through these and from there down to the rail on either side; these are the boom-topping-lifts.

From the same place hitch a block on either side, staple other blocks in the waterways, reeve lines through these and belay to the monkey-rail, for the spanker-boom-sheet.

That completes the rigging of the simple model, for the base and finishing details turn to Chapter X.

CHAPTER VIII

THE SPARS PERFECTED

In this chapter will be given details by which the spars and their fittings may be made, perhaps not quite perfect, but more nearly approaching that ideal state.

Lower-masts

Dimensions of these and all the spars will be as given in chapter VI, and the rigging plan.

These masts in our ship would be built of several spars joined together with iron bands, of which there would be about 20 below the top and 7 above. These may be painted on, but paper bands first glued on look better. Between the bands cut little V shaped notches, or chappeling, except on the fore-quarter where there is a smooth strip to take the chafe off the courses; this extends two-thirds the way down.

The lower end where it passes through the deck will be eight-sided and will there be wedged, with a mast-coat to keep the water out. This lashes round the mast above the wedges and round the mast coaming. This can be simulated with a quarter round celluloid band fitting tightly to the mast at the deck.

Instead of the nails on the foreside of the masts there will be iron bands with bull's-eyes bolted to them.

There will be no holes in the masts for the futtock shrouds or trusses, instead for the futtock-shrouds there will be a band with eyes in it, as shown in Fig. LXVIII. On a small model this may be imitated by a piece of wire with two or six eyes in it, the two ends of which are twisted together and sunk into the fore side of the mast.

The cheeks will be as before (Fig. LX) but bolted on a bit lower to make room for the trestle-trees which are bolted to the mast above them. (Be careful of the angle of the upper edge of the cheeks so that the tops lie horizontal). Trestle-trees, cross-trees and top may be made all in one as shown in the same illustration. Note that in this case there is room for the top-mast to slide up through the top as it would in reality, and that there are holes or hooks in the edge of the top for the buntline and other blocks to hook to. The quarter-round bolsters are for the shrouds to lie on.

The lower-mast head will be squared as before and to it will be fitted the cap to lie horizontal, the fore part having a hole to take the top-mast. Across the cap and mast-head should be bolted a strap to hang the blocks of the lifts, this should be about quarter-round as shown at h.

The design of the trusses can be seen at j. One band goes round the mast and the double band round the yard, with a double swivel between, so that the yard can swing horizontally or vertically. As the vertical swing is not needed, a simplified but sufficiently good looking truss for a small model can be made from thin sheet brass doubled or flattened copper wire, as shown at k.

From the mast, close under the top a short piece of chain will help to support the yard. It is the sling, l.

Top-masts

The top-masts will be the same as previously described, except that the lower end will not be squared, but have a hole through it to take the fid (bolt) to prevent it slipping through the top when in position. (See Fig. LXIX, a.) At the upper end it will be square and have

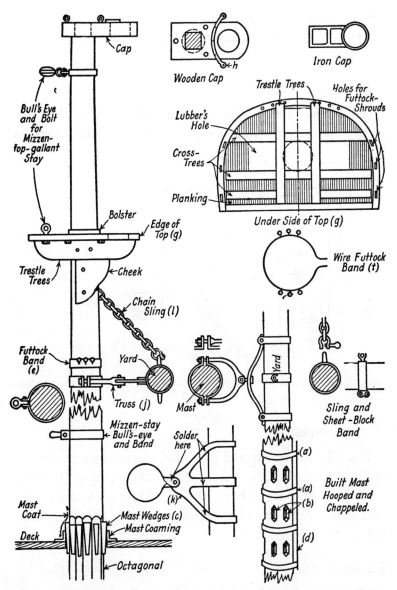

Cap

Wooden Cap

←h

Iron Cap

Bull's Eye and Bolt for Mizzen-top-gallant Stay

Trestle Trees

Holes for Futtock-Shrouds

Lubber's Hole

Cross-Trees

Planking

Under Side of Top (g)

Bolster

Edge of Top (g)

Trestle Trees

Cheek

Wire Futtock Band (t)

Chain Sling (l)

Futtock Band (e)

Yard

Truss (j)

Mast

Yard

Sling and Sheet-Block Band

Mizzen-stay Bull's-eye and Band

Solder here

(k)

(a)

(a)

Built Mast Hooped and Chappeled.

(b)

Mast Coat

Mast Wedges (c)

Mast Coaming

Deck

(d)

Octagonal

Fig. LXVIII.—Details of the lowermasts, with their fittings.   Scale 1/8".

trestle trees fitted to it, b, fore-and-aft and above this a built-up cross-trees, c, and chafing band, with a small bolster for the rigging.

Top-gallant-masts

These masts will be as in chapter VI except that they should be fidded instead of being stepped into the crosstrees.

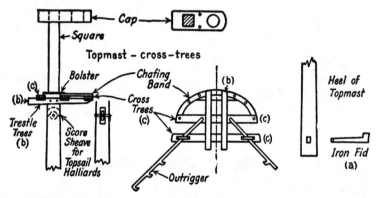

Fig. LXIX.—Details of the topmast-heads and heels with their fittings. Scale 1/12".

Try-sail-mast

Exactly as for model A. This mast has that name because that was the name of the sails at one time that were hooped to it. There were similar masts at the main and fore. Iron travellers have now been substituted for these spars.

Lower-yards

These yards to be correct will need quite a lot of fittings, but their shape remains the same. The design of the trusses and slings was given in Fig. LXVIII, and may also be seen in Fig. LXX at a. At the yard-arm stops there will be brace-bands, c. These have an eye above for the topping-lift-blocks, and one abaft for the braces (fore-side at the cross-jack). They can be regular iron bands with eyebolts, or made as suggested for the futtock-bands. At the extreme end there should be a small band, or a bolt for the reef-tackles and flemish-horses, or if the model is to have studding-sail booms, then boom irons, h, and another farther in, i. (Note, paragraph on studdingsail booms). Along the top of the yard there will be the jack-stays, these, as the name suggests, are for Jack to hang onto when standing on the foot-ropes; they are also used to make the heads of the sails fast to. They are iron bars running through iron bolts. A simple way to make them is with fine wire laid along the yard, the ends being bent sharply and driven in, and with several bent-pin staples to hold them in line along the top of the yard.

From these bolts will be hung the foot-ropes, e, with their stirrups, t, and the Flemish-horses, g. The Flemish-horses were as a rule only found on the topsail-yards, but the lower-yards also had them sometimes.

Immediately inside the brace-bands are sheaves (pulleys) for the topsail-sheets seen at k, in later ships these were sometimes bolted on abaft the yard. There should also be a lead for the sheet near the middle of the yard, z.

Top-sail-yards

The fittings for these will be seen in Fig. LXX. In the middle where they come to the mast there will be a wooden saddle bolted on, cut to the round of the mast; through these and the yards will be bolted the parrals, a, which hinge on the one side, are clipped round the mast, when in position, and bolted together on the other, see b. The parrals would be covered with leather, well greased.

For the tie of the halliards there will be an iron band with an eye-bolt round the middle of the yard, d.

At the yard-arms there will be brace bands, c, as for the lower yards. They will also be fitted with footropes, and jackstays, and studding-sail-boom irons if desired.

Top-gallant-yards

These will be the same as the top-sail-yards, except that Flemish-horses are not required.

Royal and Skysail-yards

The same as the top-gallant-yards, except for the different arrangement of the footropes. The footropes were at one time all called horses, hence the term "stirrup."

Bowsprit

The bowsprit will be as shown in Fig. LIX, but should in addition have cleats, called bees, on either side to retain the fore-top-mast-stay; these butt right up to the cap. From the eye of that stay on either side to short stanchions set in the knight-heads, there should be hand-ropes, for men going out on the boom to hold to. (See Fig. LXXI.)

Jib-boom

This may have the iron bands with bolts for the boom-guys, shown in Fig. LIX and should have footropes from the edge of the cap to the end of the boom, on either side, with a stirrup at the first stop.

Dolphin-striker

This is also shown in detail in Fig. LIX.

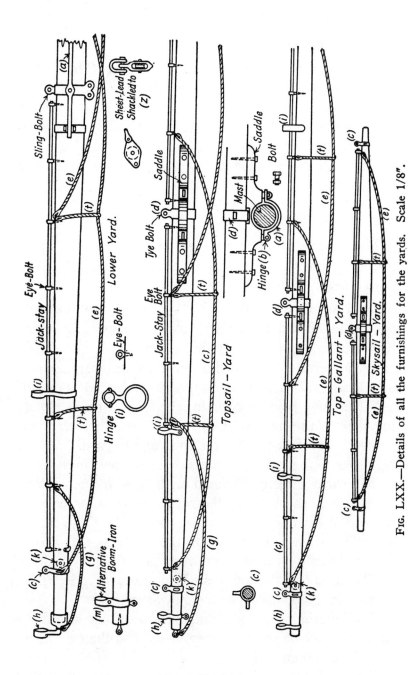

FIG. LXX.—Details of all the furnishings for the yards. Scale 1/8".

Sling-Bolt

Sheet-Lead Shackled to (z)

Eye-Bolt

Jack-stay

Eye-Bolt

Eye-Bolt

Lower Yard.

Hinge (i)

Alternative Boom-Iron

(m)

Saddle

Tye Bolt (d)

Eye Bolt

Jack-Stay Bolt

Topsail - Yard.

Mast

Saddle

Bolt

(d)

Hinge (b)

(a)

Top - Gallant - Yard.

Skysail - Yard.

[121]

Spanker-gaff and boom

These will be as previously described, except that bands with eyes will be substituted for holes and jaws for the wire eye at the butt end of the gaff and a goose-neck or swivel-eye on the end of the boom, working on a band round the trysail-mast. (See Fig. LXXI.)

There should also be a belaying-pin-band round the mizzen-mast.

Studding-sail-booms

The Sovereign of the Seas carried studding-sails (pronounced stu'n's'l) extending from the royal, top-gallant, topsail and lower yards.

The sails were fastened to light yards which hung from booms, as shown on the sail plan on page 136. The booms lay along the top of the regular yards and slid in and out in iron rings called boom-irons and were secured by a lashing at their inner end, whether rigged in or out.

When they were rigged in, their heels came almost together at the middle of the yards and their ends extended a few feet beyond the ends of the yards. When rigged out, their heels came almost to the inner irons.

The yards came right down on deck with the sail, and were hoisted to blocks at the permanent yard-arms. To the end of each boom a block was secured by a grommet (rope ring) for the sheet of the studding-sail above. These blocks were sent down when the sails were unbent.

The sheets of the lower studding-sails were extended by swinging booms, from the bulwarks.

The lengths of the studding-sail-booms are about the same as one half the yard they lie on, and their diameter a shade less than one half, say $\frac{3}{7}$ths.

Several forms of yard-arm boom-irons were used, that

shown at h. in Fig. LXX, either a cap to go over the yard end or a bolt to go in it, is the most likely for our ship, but that shown at m is rather easier and neater. The inner boom-iron was hinged so that the top half of the upper band opened and clipped over the boom, to allow

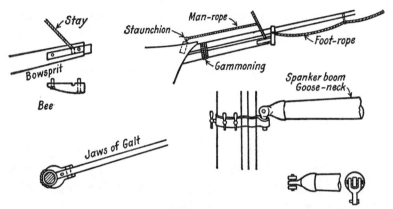

Fɪɢ. LXXI.—Fastening the fore-topmast-stay to the bowsprit-end with a bee. Jib-boom manropes and footropes. Gaff jaws and spanker-boom gooseneck.

of easily shipping and unshipping, as with a yard parral.

It is quite optional on the part of the reader whether he puts these booms and their irons on his ship or not; they add to its completeness, but, to my thinking, detract from its smart appearance.

CHAPTER IX

RIGGING MODEL B

THE order and method of rigging the elaborate model B will be the same as for the simplified model, described in Chapter VII, but it will have to be more carefully done with the right kind of fittings, or something approaching them.

Deadeyes

To commence with the shrouds and backstays will have to be set up with deadeyes, the upper ones turned into the ends of the rigging and the lower fastened to chain-plates. These may be seen in Fig. LXXII. There are so many of these deadeyes that it is well to find out the easiest method of making them, according to the tools available.

The sizes are some 16 in. dia. (actual measurement) for the shrouds, 10 in. for the top-mast-back-stays, and 6 in. for the rest. These seem quite big, but will be found very small to work at when brought down to scale.

The best thing to make them of is box-wood, and the easiest round lengths of celluloid, such as knitting needles. Each one is a flat circular disc, with three holes in the form of a triangle, and a groove round it with the edges rounded off.

The grooves can be cut and the shoulders rounded in a lathe, a treadle fretsaw machine, or hand fretsaw; they should then be cut off, have the holes bored and the edges rounded with a small file. The celluloid ones can be cut

[124]

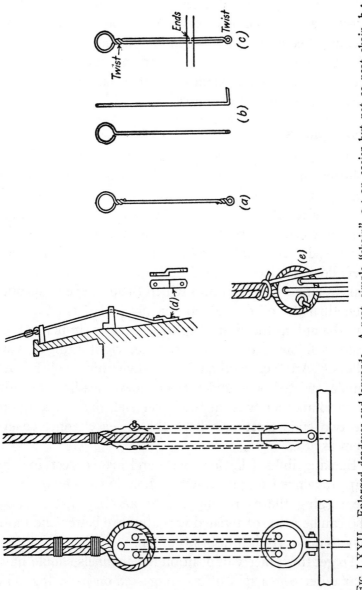

Fig. LXXII.—Enlarged deadeyes and lanyards. A neat, simple "chain", a.; an easier but not so neat chain, b.; a better method of making the chains, c. Fastening off the end of the lanyard, e. A backing link, d.

with a knife, giving it a slicing movement rather than a direct pressure; the holes can then be bored with a blunt darning needle set in a wooden handle, heated in a flame. I have made many thus and never had one catch alight, but one must always be careful when handling celluloid because it is highly inflamable.

Chain-plates

Having made the deadeyes, the lower ones have to be fastened in position. In Fig. LXXII a. shows how the chain-plates should be made for this model, using soft copper wire which is laid in the groove of the deadeye twisted close underneath and has a small eye in the lower end. A simpler method, seen at b., which, however, does not look so good, is to use spring brass wire, make a ring in one end into which the deadeye is sprung, then turn the other end up sharply and drive that end into the hull at the right height. These chain-plates hold quite well but are not so near the right thing as the others. Another method is to have thin copper wire double, twisted once under the deadeye, leading straight down to another twist at the lower end, then back again, the two ends meeting where the lower channel covers them as at c.

Backing links (d.) look well and are correct for the ship; they are iron plates with a hole in each end, giving the rigging the extra support of another bolt. These also can be made of twisted wire, but are better and more easy to make from thin brass or tin.

To get these nicely in position the channels should have their outer edges split off as suggested on page 48. The deadeyes must sit close to the upper channel, and the lower ends must be on a straight line.

The upper deadeyes must be neatly seized into the ends

of the shrouds and backstays, with one or two seizings of thin sewing silk or cotton, neatly knotting the ends with a touch of glue so that they can be cut off close. The end of the shroud should come up to the left hand, looking from inboard—out.

The center hole of the upper deadeye must be up and that of the lower deadeye, down.

For the lanyards use linen or silk thread of rather less

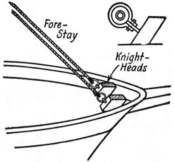

Fig. LXXIII.—Turning the ends of the fore-stay up through bull's-eyes bolted to the knight-heads.

than one half the thickness of the shroud, put a neat knot in one end, reeve the other end through the lower hole of the upper deadeye; under the end part of the shroud; through the corresponding hole in the lower dead-eye; through the center ones and so on; finishing off with a clove hitch round the shroud, close above the deadeye, see e. which is a view from inboard-out.

The Stays

The stays will lead much as previously described. The fore stays will set up to bull's-eyes bolted to the knight-heads. (See Fig. LXXIII). The main stay to similar eyes attached by iron bands to the bolster of the fore-topsail-sheet-bitts or forward fife-rail. The main-top-mast-preventer-and mizzen-stays lead through the bull's-eyes strapped abaft the fore and main masts, from thence to other bull's-eyes bolted to the deck directly beneath.

The main-top-mast and mizzen top-gallant-stays, will lead through bull's-eyes underneath the caps at the fore and main and set up to bolts in the tops.

The other stays will be as for the simplified model.

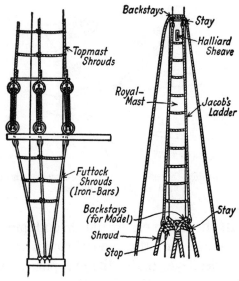

FIG. LXXIV.—The topmast-shrouds and futtock-shrouds. The Jacob's ladder abaft the royal-mast.

Top-mast-rigging

This rigging will have to set up with dead-eyes to others in the ends of the futtock-shrouds, as with the lower shrouds but using 10 in. dead-eyes.

The lower deadeyes will be twisted into thin copper wire as was done below, the other ends of the wire being fastened to the futtock-bands; three on a side, with the deadeyes sitting snug to the top. On a small scale model it is really neater to take the wire through the mast and up to the corresponding deadeyes on the other side, just painting a band on. The upper deadeyes will be turned into the ends of the rigging and set up with lanyards as before. (See Fig. LXXIV.)

Top-gallant-rigging

This will not require deadeyes, but will have eyes spliced in the lower ends by which with small lanyards it will be set up to battens seized under the topmast rigging, below the cross-trees.

Jacob's ladder

From the top-gallant-mast-head to the royal-mast-head there should be a jacob's ladder, abaft the royal-mast, (See Fig. LXXIV.)

Yard Lifts

The lower-yard-topping-lifts, will be gun-tackle purchases with the lower block hooked to the brace-band and the upper to the iron across the lower cap, the end leading down to the fife-rail.

The other lifts will be single cords, from the brace-bands to the cross-trees and mast heads, to which their other ends are lashed.

Halliards

A top-sail-yard-halliard is a chain from the center of the yard through a score with a sheave in the mast under the cross-trees, then down abaft to a large flat iron block, this chain is long enough to allow the yard to come down to the cap. Through the latter block is rove a long chain which is bolted to the deck on

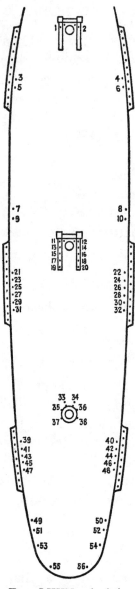

Fig. LXXV.—A belay-
ing-pin plan, showing
where the ends of the
running gear come to the
belaying-pin rails.

BELAYING-PIN PLAN

Positions in which the braces, halliards, etc. are belayed.

1-2. Fore-yard-lifts.
3. Fore-topsail-halliards.
4. Fore - top - gallant - hal - liards.
5. Fore-royal-halliards.
6. Fore-skysail-halliards.
7-8. Fore-topsail-yard-braces.
9-10. Fore-yard-braces.
11-12. Main-yard-lifts.
13-14. Mizzen-topsail-braces.
15-16. Cross-jack-braces.
17-18. Mizzen-royal-braces.
19-20. Mizzen-skysail-braces.
21-22. Fore-top-gallant-braces.
23-24. Fore-royal-braces.
25-26. Fore-skysail-braces.
27. Main - top - gallant - hal - liards.
28. Main-topsail-halliards.
29. Main-skysail-halliards.
30. Main-royal-halliards.
31-32. Mizzen - top - gallant braces.

33-34. Cross-jack-yard-lifts.
35. Spanker-gaff-throat-hal - liards.
36. Spanker-gaff-peak-hal - liards.
37-38. Spanker-boom-quarter - lifts.
39-40. Main-top-gallant-yard - braces.
41-42. Main-royal-yard-braces.
43-44. Main-skysail-braces.
45. Mizzen-topsail-halliards.
46. Mizzen-top-gallant-hal - liards.
47. Mizzen-royal-halliards.
48. Mizzen-skysail-halliards.
49-50. Spanker-gaff-vangs.
51-52. Main - topsail - yard - braces.
53-54. Main-yard-braces.
55-56. Spanker-boom-sheets.

one side and has a double block on the other, another double block is shackled to a bolt in the deck and a tackle rove through these, the fall leading through a single block also bolted to the deck and from there belayed to the pin-rail. This tackle should be amply long enough to allow the yard to hoist and lower. The end of the chain is to starboard and the purchase to port at the fore, and reverses this order at each mast.

The top-gallant-halliards are chain where they run through the mast, to the chain is spliced a long rope which comes down to the purchase, as described in Chapter VII.

The royal and skysail-halliards, will be as there described, but seized to the bolts in the yards and all, of course, properly belayed to pins in the rail.

Braces

The braces will all be rove off as before described, but the ends must be all brought to the deck and properly belayed. Have the lead blocks seized to the eyes of the stays, very close up to the mast-heads, so that if the yards were hoisted the braces would run clear of them; you will find that at the top-gallant-mast-head other blocks will be needed under and slightly abaft the rigging, to make them lead clear, down abaft the masts. The upper braces have fair-leads or seizing trucks seized to the backstays, to prevent them chafing and swinging about. Some of these will be at the cross-tree outriggers, and there should be a whole row of them seized to the backstays at about 15 feet from the deck. Small black beads serve the purpose very well.

The positions in which all the ropes should be belayed is shown in Fig. LXXV.

The topsail-braces, in addition to the purchase previously described, should have a single block (whip) purchase on their ends.

Where the cords are too heavy to be rove off (threaded) with a needle, the best way is to get a piece of cobbler's wax, and put a stiff point on them with this, shaving the point down, if necessary. For the lanyards, of which a number of the same length are needed, dip the

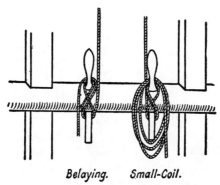

Belaying.   Small-Coil.

Fig. LXXVI.—Belaying a rope.

ends in thin glue, wipe off the surplus and leave them to dry.

Imitation splices can be made by pointing the end of the cord with a sharp knife, touching it with glue, twisting it onto the standing part, and neatly binding with thin silk.

Belaying is sometimes quite tricky work, especially when one has to work across a crowded deck. For this purpose the belaying instrument described in Chapter II is valuable, with a pair of pointed tweezers to help. The rope must be taken under the pin, across and over, under again and finished, as a rule, with a hitch. A spot of glue on the pins will retain the turns until the next is made. The ropes are seldom hitched at sea, but are occasionally in bad weather, thus are permissible.

If coils are desired, and they certainly give a finish, the end of the ropes should be wound round a piece of stick and laid on the belaying pin with a touch of glue to keep the turns from uncoiling. An easy plan, where it is possible to employ it, as with the braces, is to start by making a small coil, hitching it to the pin, and then reeving the rope in reverse, finishing at the mast head, yard or elsewhere as the case may be.

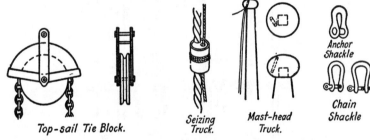

Top-sail Tie Block.   Seizing Truck.   Mast-head Truck.   Anchor Shackle   Chain Shackle

Fig. LXXVII.—Details of several small parts.

Spanker-gaff and boom

The gear for these will be as described with the addition of whips on the vangs and boom-topping-lifts.

This, so far as I can remember, will be sufficient guide to make your model a really fine piece of work, though there are many niceties that might be observed, if the scale is large enough to warrant them. I allude to such work as serving the ropes where the chafe comes, splicing, having sheaves in the blocks and so forth.

Details for such work, may be found in many old books such as *The Art of Rigging, Young Officers Sheet Anchor* and in volumes of *The Shipmodeler* published by the Ship Model Makers' Club.

SAILS

It is not the function of this book to describe a model with sails. Nevertheless plans of the sails with the running gear for handling them are given.

These plans should be sufficient to enable those experienced in such work to add the sails to their models, but the inexperienced are not advised to attempt them without further information.

For the benefit of those who want to add sails to their models, the author has made a sail plan with many details for fixing and rigging them. To the same scale of $\frac{1}{12}$ in.—1 ft.

Also $\frac{1}{8}$ in. scale plan showing the position in which all the ropes are belayed.

See advertisement at the end of the book.

The reader should decide before starting the rigging, whether he is going to give the model sails or not, because of the extra blocks and gear required.

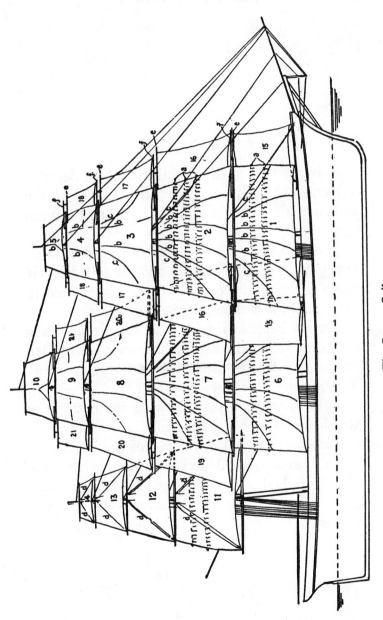

The Square Sails.

THE SQUARE-SAILS OF THE SOVEREIGN
OF THE SEAS

1. Fore - course (or fore-sail).
2. Fore-top-sail.
3. Fore-top-gallant-sail.
4. Fore-royal.
5. Fore-sky-sail.
6. Main-course.
7. Main-top-sail.
8. Main-top-gallant-sail.
9. Main-royal.
10. Main-sky-sail.
11. Mizzen-top-sail.
12. Mizzen-top-gallant-sail.
13. Mizzen-royal.
14. Mizzen-sky-sail.
15. Fore-lower-studding-sails.
16. Fore-top-mast-studding-sails.
17. Fore-top-gallant-studding-sails.
18. Fore-royal-studding-sails.
19. Main-top-mast-studding-sails.
20. Main-top-gallant-studding-sails.
21. Main-royal-studding-sails

a. Reef-bands and points.
b. Bunt-lines. Shown at the fore only.
c. Leech-lines. Ditto.
d. Clew-garnets. Abaft the sails. Shown at the mizzen only.
e. Studding-sail-yards.
f. Studding-sail-booms.

The Fore-and-Aft Sails.

THE FORE-AND-AFT SAILS OF THE SOVEREIGN
OF THE SEAS

15. Flying-jib.
16. Outer-jib.
17. Inner-jib.
18. Fore-top-mast-stay-sail.
19. Main-royal-stay-sail.
20. Main-top-gallant-stay-sail.
21. Main-top-mast-stay-sail.
22. Mizzen-top-gallant-stay-sail.
23. Mizzen-top-mast-stay-sail.
24. Spanker or driver.

Running - Gear for Handling
these Sails

a. Halliards.
b. Down-hauls.
c. Sheets (jib-sheets double).

NOTE—The number used and cut of these sails varied considerably, between one ship and another.

CHAPTER X

FINISHING TOUCHES

PRESUMABLY by now the model is built, has her deck furnishings and rigging in place and painted; there now remains to make the base and add the last few pieces.

The base or stand for the model may be of any shape and size desired. The design given in Fig. LXXVIII being one that the author has found practical and suitable.

Any hard-wood may be used, oak being perhaps the most suitable, because it always seems to me that oak and these ships belong together.

The flat part should be about 13x4¾x¾ in. with the top edges champhered. The uprights should be of the same wood 4⅜x2½x¾ in. The pattern given may be traced on them and the design cut with a fretsaw and lightly carved, or the outer edges may be a curve only. The inside edges are to fit snug to the hull, with a slot for the keel, when the uprights are about 7 in. apart. They are best morticed onto the base block but may be glued and nailed only.

The base may be stained, varnished or polished.

An anchor will be wanted for each bow. The shanks and arms can be cast in bronze, white metal or lead, or can be bought ready made. Bronze anchors are, of course, the nicest but are a lot of trouble to make, are a little more expensive to buy and are hardly necessary because they have to be painted black.

If desired to make one of copper or bronze, it can be

done from ⅛ in. square copper such as nails, by filing to shape and soldering together.

A lead one may be cast by making it first in wood, taking a plaster of paris mold of this, and then pouring the lead into the mold. They may also be made from a piece of ⅛ in. thick sheet lead, such as a piece of gas pipe, by cutting out the shape, flat, as shown in Fig.

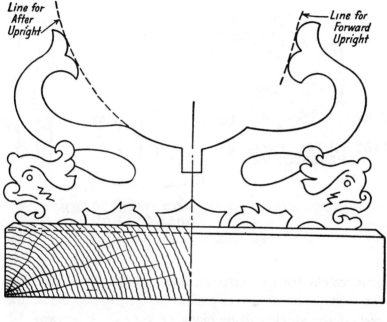

Fig. LXXVIII.—The forward and after uprights for the base or stand. This drawing is under-scale. The width of the base is 4 1/2″.

LXXIX, then twisting the two arms and hammering them back into square shape.

The shank should be 1⅝ in. long, a full ⅛ in. square where it meets the crown, tapering to the end, where it is flattened and bored for the ring, which is at a right angle to the arms. The arms should be 1⅜ in. across and the flukes ⁵⁄₁₆ in. across, by ⅜ in. deep.

[141]

The stock is made of wood shaped as shown in the same illustration, the flat side being the upper. It is $1\frac{1}{8}$ in. long, has a square hole in the middle to take the shank. When shaped, split it in half, lengthwise, put it on the shank at right angles with the arms, then glue the two halves together and bind them with thread in

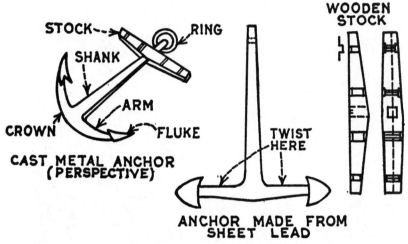

STOCK RING SHANK ARM CROWN FLUKE

CAST METAL ANCHOR (PERSPECTIVE)

WOODEN STOCK

TWIST HERE

ANCHOR MADE FROM SHEET LEAD

FIG. LXXIX.—Anchor details.

grooves cut for the purpose, these bindings will look like the iron bands of a real anchor when painted black, the rest of the stock will be black or very dark brown.

There now remains to shackle the anchors to their chains, which with the simple model are stapled with a pin into the hawse-pipes, and with model B the chains are brought up the hawse pipes, round the windlass and into the spurling-gates. The anchors are then fastened to the catheads by the stoppers and to the staples in the deck by the shank-painters.

The links of the cable for the $\frac{1}{12}$ in. scale model should be about 12 to the inch and should, of course be painted

black. The inside of the hawsepipes should be scarlet.
The shank-painters should be chain but unless you have
a very small kind, it is better to use cord.

The rudder should have small chains lashed to the
counter, so that the rudder can be worked with tackles
if the steering-gear breaks down. The middle of this
chain is shackled to a long eye bolt in the rudder just
above the waterline, each part is then seized to an eye

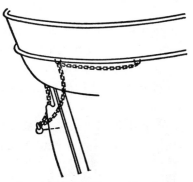

Fig. LXXX.—The rudder chains.

bolt in the counter about half way from midships, with
sufficient slack to allow the rudder to swing, the ends are
seized to other bolts at the same level (under the molding) at the quarters. (See Fig. LXXX.)

It was advised in Chapter IV that the boats be left
until now. The davits should be shipped, either through
the rail for model A or close to it outside on model B;
the guys made fast; the boats hoisted in position by their
tackles, and lashed.

If the scale of the model permits, there should be a
life-bouy hung in beckets to the taffrail on each side of
the poop. A life-buoy is in reality made of cork, covered
with canvas, with four canvas straps holding a slack
cord, round it. It always has the name of the ship and

her port of registry painted on it. The becket is made of two canvas strips seized to the handrail, so that it can readily be slipped out, when wanted.

FIG. LXXXI.—A side-light and screen.

A vessel of this period would have to carry navigation lights, commonly called side-lights, to warn other vessels of her approach. A lantern showing a red light would be placed on the port side and one showing a green light on the starboard.

These lanterns would be placed in screens projecting three feet beyond the light, to prevent the light showing

FIG. LXXXII.—A life-buoy and becket.

across the bow. Their usual place in the earlier ships was in the mizzen rigging above the level of the boats. Fig. LXXXI shows the starboard side-light and its screen. The lantern itself would be about 18 in. high and of quarter-round shape, fitted to drop onto an iron cleat at the back of the screen which would be seized to the mizzen rigging.

The house (company) flag, can be painted, with water

colors on thin silk and is the better for having the edges touched with clear shellac or gum to prevent fraying. It is a swallow-tail with three Vs, blue to the mast, red and white. The hoist (edge to the mast) is glued to the bight

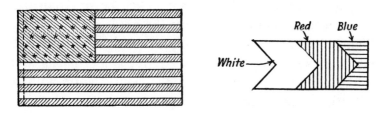

FIG. LXXXIII.—The flags.

of a length of fine silk, this is then put over the mast head and the truck jammed down over it, making sure that the flag is right up as far as it will go, the ends brought down inside the rigging and made fast to it at the deck.

The ensign, is the usual American flag, except that there were only 31 states at that time so there will be only 31 stars on it. The arrangement of the stars seems to have varied at that time, but that shown in Fig. LXXXIII is as good as any. The halliards will be put on as with the house flag, the end being taken through the small eye at the gaff end and belayed to the rail or hitched to the boom.

Look well over the whole model; set her in the base with the keel level and the masts upright. See that the yards are truly horizontal, hanging as low as the lifts will allow and fairly squared across the hull.

Some model makers prefer to have the yards braced-up as if she were sailing with a leading wind. If the model is chiefly to be looked at broadside-on this is rather more effective and is the plan the writer adopts with a model that has the sails set but, when there are no sails, a real ship almost invariably has her yards squared, thus it is not so correct.

If, however, they are wanted this way, the lower yards should be at an angle with the keel of about 4 points (45°) and the yards above should each be squared in a little until the skysail yards have the angle of about 65°.

Take a look aloft and alow to see that there are no bare spots or misplaced paint spots. Dirty fingermarks and the like can be removed from the white paint with a small stiff brush dipped in turpentine or any cleaning fluid.

The stars and stripes being hoisted, the ship is complete, a thing of beauty and grace, an ornament to any home and a reminder of the days when bold Americans ventured forth in their unsurpassable clippers, and swiftly carried this flag to the far ends of the earth.

Now sails are past; and still the sail ship grips
The carpenter with wood-dust on his hair,
And down below he fashions from slim strips
The rakish models of the ships that were.

—CHARLES NORMAN.

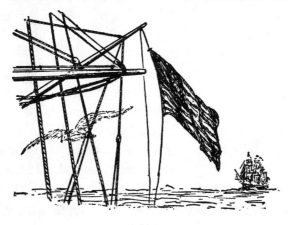

INDEX

INDEX

INDEX

INDEX

A CATALOG OF SELECTED
DOVER BOOKS
IN ALL FIELDS OF INTEREST

A CATALOG OF SELECTED DOVER
BOOKS IN ALL FIELDS OF INTEREST

CONCERNING THE SPIRITUAL IN ART, Wassily Kandinsky. Pioneering work by father of abstract art. Thoughts on color theory, nature of art. Analysis of earlier masters. 12 illustrations. 80pp. of text. 5⅜ x 8½.   23411-8 Pa. $4.95

ANIMALS: 1,419 Copyright-Free Illustrations of Mammals, Birds, Fish, Insects, etc., Jim Harter (ed.). Clear wood engravings present, in extremely lifelike poses, over 1,000 species of animals. One of the most extensive pictorial sourcebooks of its kind. Captions. Index. 284pp. 9 x 12.   23766-4 Pa. $14.95

CELTIC ART: The Methods of Construction, George Bain. Simple geometric techniques for making Celtic interlacements, spirals, Kells-type initials, animals, humans, etc. Over 500 illustrations. 160pp. 9 x 12. (USO)   22923-8 Pa. $9.95

AN ATLAS OF ANATOMY FOR ARTISTS, Fritz Schider. Most thorough reference work on art anatomy in the world. Hundreds of illustrations, including selections from works by Vesalius, Leonardo, Goya, Ingres, Michelangelo, others. 593 illustrations. 192pp. 7⅛ x 10¼.   20241-0 Pa. $9.95

CELTIC HAND STROKE-BY-STROKE (Irish Half-Uncial from "The Book of Kells"): An Arthur Baker Calligraphy Manual, Arthur Baker. Complete guide to creating each letter of the alphabet in distinctive Celtic manner. Covers hand position, strokes, pens, inks, paper, more. Illustrated. 48pp. 8¼ x 11.   24336-2 Pa. $3.95

EASY ORIGAMI, John Montroll. Charming collection of 32 projects (hat, cup, pelican, piano, swan, many more) specially designed for the novice origami hobbyist. Clearly illustrated easy-to-follow instructions insure that even beginning papercrafters will achieve successful results. 48pp. 8¼ x 11.   27298-2 Pa. $3.50

THE COMPLETE BOOK OF BIRDHOUSE CONSTRUCTION FOR WOOD-WORKERS, Scott D. Campbell. Detailed instructions, illustrations, tables. Also data on bird habitat and instinct patterns. Bibliography. 3 tables. 63 illustrations in 15 figures. 48pp. 5¼ x 8½.   24407-5 Pa. $2.50

BLOOMINGDALE'S ILLUSTRATED 1886 CATALOG: Fashions, Dry Goods and Housewares, Bloomingdale Brothers. Famed merchants' extremely rare catalog depicting about 1,700 products: clothing, housewares, firearms, dry goods, jewelry, more. Invaluable for dating, identifying vintage items. Also, copyright-free graphics for artists, designers. Co-published with Henry Ford Museum & Greenfield Village. 160pp. 8¼ x 11.   25780-0 Pa. $10.95

HISTORIC COSTUME IN PICTURES, Braun & Schneider. Over 1,450 costumed figures in clearly detailed engravings—from dawn of civilization to end of 19th century. Captions. Many folk costumes. 256pp. 8⅜ x 11¾.   23150-X Pa. $12.95

CATALOG OF DOVER BOOKS

STICKLEY CRAFTSMAN FURNITURE CATALOGS, Gustav Stickley and L. & J. G. Stickley. Beautiful, functional furniture in two authentic catalogs from 1910. 594 illustrations, including 277 photos, show settles, rockers, armchairs, reclining chairs, bookcases, desks, tables. 183pp. 6½ x 9¼.   23838-5 Pa. $11.95

AMERICAN LOCOMOTIVES IN HISTORIC PHOTOGRAPHS: 1858 to 1949, Ron Ziel (ed.). A rare collection of 126 meticulously detailed official photographs, called "builder portraits," of American locomotives that majestically chronicle the rise of steam locomotive power in America. Introduction. Detailed captions. xi + 129pp. 9 x 12.   27393-8 Pa. $13.95

AMERICA'S LIGHTHOUSES: An Illustrated History, Francis Ross Holland, Jr. Delightfully written, profusely illustrated fact-filled survey of over 200 American lighthouses since 1716. History, anecdotes, technological advances, more. 240pp. 8 x 10¾.
25576-X Pa. $12.95

TOWARDS A NEW ARCHITECTURE, Le Corbusier. Pioneering manifesto by founder of "International School." Technical and aesthetic theories, views of industry, economics, relation of form to function, "mass-production split" and much more. Profusely illustrated. 320pp. 6⅛ x 9¼. (USO)   25023-7 Pa. $9.95

HOW THE OTHER HALF LIVES, Jacob Riis. Famous journalistic record, exposing poverty and degradation of New York slums around 1900, by major social reformer. 100 striking and influential photographs. 233pp. 10 x 7⅞.
22012-5 Pa. $11.95

FRUIT KEY AND TWIG KEY TO TREES AND SHRUBS, William M. Harlow. One of the handiest and most widely used identification aids. Fruit key covers 120 deciduous and evergreen species; twig key 160 deciduous species. Easily used. Over 300 photographs. 126pp. 5⅜ x 8½.   20511-8 Pa. $3.95

COMMON BIRD SONGS, Dr. Donald J. Borror. Songs of 60 most common U.S. birds: robins, sparrows, cardinals, bluejays, finches, more—arranged in order of increasing complexity. Up to 9 variations of songs of each species.
Cassette and manual 99911-4 $8.95

ORCHIDS AS HOUSE PLANTS, Rebecca Tyson Northen. Grow cattleyas and many other kinds of orchids—in a window, in a case, or under artificial light. 63 illustrations. 148pp. 5⅜ x 8½.   23261-1 Pa. $5.95

MONSTER MAZES, Dave Phillips. Masterful mazes at four levels of difficulty. Avoid deadly perils and evil creatures to find magical treasures. Solutions for all 32 exciting illustrated puzzles. 48pp. 8¼ x 11.   26005-4 Pa. $2.95

MOZART'S DON GIOVANNI (DOVER OPERA LIBRETTO SERIES), Wolfgang Amadeus Mozart. Introduced and translated by Ellen H. Bleiler. Standard Italian libretto, with complete English translation. Convenient and thoroughly portable—an ideal companion for reading along with a recording or the performance itself. Introduction. List of characters. Plot summary. 121pp. 5¼ x 8½.
24944-1 Pa. $3.95

TECHNICAL MANUAL AND DICTIONARY OF CLASSICAL BALLET, Gail Grant. Defines, explains, comments on steps, movements, poses and concepts. 15-page pictorial section. Basic book for student, viewer. 127pp. 5⅜ x 8½.
21843-0 Pa. $4.95

THE CLARINET AND CLARINET PLAYING, David Pino. Lively, comprehensive work features suggestions about technique, musicianship, and musical interpretation, as well as guidelines for teaching, making your own reeds, and preparing for public performance. Includes an intriguing look at clarinet history. "A godsend," The Clarinet, Journal of the International Clarinet Society. Appendixes. 7 illus. 320pp. 5⅜ x 8½. 40270-3 Pa. $9.95

HOLLYWOOD GLAMOR PORTRAITS, John Kobal (ed.). 145 photos from 1926-49. Harlow, Gable, Bogart, Bacall; 94 stars in all. Full background on photographers, technical aspects. 160pp. 8⅜ x 11¼. 23352-9 Pa. $12.95

THE ANNOTATED CASEY AT THE BAT: A Collection of Ballads about the Mighty Casey/Third, Revised Edition, Martin Gardner (ed.). Amusing sequels and parodies of one of America's best-loved poems: Casey's Revenge, Why Casey Whiffed, Casey's Sister at the Bat, others. 256pp. 5⅜ x 8½. 28598-7 Pa. $8.95

THE RAVEN AND OTHER FAVORITE POEMS, Edgar Allan Poe. Over 40 of the author's most memorable poems: "The Bells," "Ulalume," "Israfel," "To Helen," "The Conqueror Worm," "Eldorado," "Annabel Lee," many more. Alphabetic lists of titles and first lines. 64pp. 5 3/16 x 8¼. 26685-0 Pa. $1.00

PERSONAL MEMOIRS OF U. S. GRANT, Ulysses Simpson Grant. Intelligent, deeply moving firsthand account of Civil War campaigns, considered by many the finest military memoirs ever written. Includes letters, historic photographs, maps and more. 528pp. 6⅛ x 9¼. 28587-1 Pa. $12.95

ANCIENT EGYPTIAN MATERIALS AND INDUSTRIES, A. Lucas and J. Harris. Fascinating, comprehensive, thoroughly documented text describes this ancient civilization's vast resources and the processes that incorporated them in daily life, including the use of animal products, building materials, cosmetics, perfumes and incense, fibers, glazed ware, glass and its manufacture, materials used in the mummification process, and much more. 544pp. 6⅛ x 9¼. (USO)
40446-3 Pa. $16.95

RUSSIAN STORIES/PYCCKNE PACCKA3bl: A Dual-Language Book, edited by Gleb Struve. Twelve tales by such masters as Chekhov, Tolstoy, Dostoevsky, Pushkin, others. Excellent word-for-word English translations on facing pages, plus teaching and study aids, Russian/English vocabulary, biographical/critical introductions, more. 416pp. 5⅜ x 8½. 26244-8 Pa. $9.95

PHILADELPHIA THEN AND NOW: 60 Sites Photographed in the Past and Present, Kenneth Finkel and Susan Oyama. Rare photographs of City Hall, Logan Square, Independence Hall, Betsy Ross House, other landmarks juxtaposed with contemporary views. Captures changing face of historic city. Introduction. Captions. 128pp. 8¼ x 11. 25790-8 Pa. $9.95

AIA ARCHITECTURAL GUIDE TO NASSAU AND SUFFOLK COUNTIES, LONG ISLAND, The American Institute of Architects, Long Island Chapter, and the Society for the Preservation of Long Island Antiquities. Comprehensive, well-researched and generously illustrated volume brings to life over three centuries of Long Island's great architectural heritage. More than 240 photographs with authoritative, extensively detailed captions. 176pp. 8¼ x 11. 26946-9 Pa. $14.95

NORTH AMERICAN INDIAN LIFE: Customs and Traditions of 23 Tribes, Elsie Clews Parsons (ed.). 27 fictionalized essays by noted anthropologists examine religion, customs, government, additional facets of life among the Winnebago, Crow, Zuni, Eskimo, other tribes. 480pp. 6⅛ x 9¼. 27377-6 Pa. $10.95

FRANK LLOYD WRIGHT'S DANA HOUSE, Donald Hoffmann. Pictorial essay of residential masterpiece with over 160 interior and exterior photos, plans, elevations, sketches and studies. 128pp. 9¼ x 10¾. 29120-0 Pa. $12.95

THE MALE AND FEMALE FIGURE IN MOTION: 60 Classic Photographic Sequences, Eadweard Muybridge. 60 true-action photographs of men and women walking, running, climbing, bending, turning, etc., reproduced from rare 19th-century masterpiece. vi + 121pp. 9 x 12. 24745-7 Pa. $10.95

1001 QUESTIONS ANSWERED ABOUT THE SEASHORE, N. J. Berrill and Jacquelyn Berrill. Queries answered about dolphins, sea snails, sponges, starfish, fishes, shore birds, many others. Covers appearance, breeding, growth, feeding, much more. 305pp. 5¼ x 8¼. 23366-9 Pa. $9.95

ATTRACTING BIRDS TO YOUR YARD, William J. Weber. Easy-to-follow guide offers advice on how to attract the greatest diversity of birds: birdhouses, feeders, water and waterers, much more. 96pp. 5³⁄₁₆ x 8¼. 28927-3 Pa. $2.50

MEDICINAL AND OTHER USES OF NORTH AMERICAN PLANTS: A Historical Survey with Special Reference to the Eastern Indian Tribes, Charlotte Erichsen-Brown. Chronological historical citations document 500 years of usage of plants, trees, shrubs native to eastern Canada, northeastern U.S. Also complete identifying information. 343 illustrations. 544pp. 6½ x 9¼. 25951-X Pa. $12.95

STORYBOOK MAZES, Dave Phillips. 23 stories and mazes on two-page spreads: Wizard of Oz, Treasure Island, Robin Hood, etc. Solutions. 64pp. 8¼ x 11. 23628-5 Pa. $2.95

AMERICAN NEGRO SONGS: 230 Folk Songs and Spirituals, Religious and Secular, John W. Work. This authoritative study traces the African influences of songs sung and played by black Americans at work, in church, and as entertainment. The author discusses the lyric significance of such songs as "Swing Low, Sweet Chariot," "John Henry," and others and offers the words and music for 230 songs. Bibliography. Index of Song Titles. 272pp. 6½ x 9¼. 40271-1 Pa. $9.95

MOVIE-STAR PORTRAITS OF THE FORTIES, John Kobal (ed.). 163 glamor, studio photos of 106 stars of the 1940s: Rita Hayworth, Ava Gardner, Marlon Brando, Clark Gable, many more. 176pp. 8⅜ x 11¼. 23546-7 Pa. $14.95

BENCHLEY LOST AND FOUND, Robert Benchley. Finest humor from early 30s, about pet peeves, child psychologists, post office and others. Mostly unavailable elsewhere. 73 illustrations by Peter Arno and others. 183pp. 5⅜ x 8½. 22410-4 Pa. $6.95

YEKL and THE IMPORTED BRIDEGROOM AND OTHER STORIES OF YIDDISH NEW YORK, Abraham Cahan. Film Hester Street based on Yekl (1896). Novel, other stories among first about Jewish immigrants on N.Y.'s East Side. 240pp. 5⅜ x 8½. 22427-9 Pa. $6.95

SELECTED POEMS, Walt Whitman. Generous sampling from *Leaves of Grass*. Twenty-four poems include "I Hear America Singing," "Song of the Open Road," "I Sing the Body Electric," "When Lilacs Last in the Dooryard Bloom'd," "O Captain! My Captain!"—all reprinted from an authoritative edition. Lists of titles and first lines. 128pp. 5³⁄₁₆ x 8¼. 26878-0 Pa. $1.00

THE BEST TALES OF HOFFMANN, E. T. A. Hoffmann. 10 of Hoffmann's most important stories: "Nutcracker and the King of Mice," "The Golden Flowerpot," etc. 458pp. 5⅜ x 8½. 21793-0 Pa. $9.95

FROM FETISH TO GOD IN ANCIENT EGYPT, E. A. Wallis Budge. Rich detailed survey of Egyptian conception of "God" and gods, magic, cult of animals, Osiris, more. Also, superb English translations of hymns and legends. 240 illustrations. 545pp. 5⅜ x 8½. 25803-3 Pa. $13.95

FRENCH STORIES/CONTES FRANÇAIS: A Dual-Language Book, Wallace Fowlie. Ten stories by French masters, Voltaire to Camus: "Micromegas" by Voltaire; "The Atheist's Mass" by Balzac; "Minuet" by de Maupassant; "The Guest" by Camus, six more. Excellent English translations on facing pages. Also French-English vocabulary list, exercises, more. 352pp. 5⅜ x 8½. 26443-2 Pa. $9.95

CHICAGO AT THE TURN OF THE CENTURY IN PHOTOGRAPHS: 122 Historic Views from the Collections of the Chicago Historical Society, Larry A. Viskochil. Rare large-format prints offer detailed views of City Hall, State Street, the Loop, Hull House, Union Station, many other landmarks, circa 1904-1913. Introduction. Captions. Maps. 144pp. 9⅜ x 12¼. 24656-6 Pa. $12.95

OLD BROOKLYN IN EARLY PHOTOGRAPHS, 1865-1929, William Lee Younger. Luna Park, Gravesend race track, construction of Grand Army Plaza, moving of Hotel Brighton, etc. 157 previously unpublished photographs. 165pp. 8⅞ x 11¾. 23587-4 Pa. $13.95

THE MYTHS OF THE NORTH AMERICAN INDIANS, Lewis Spence. Rich anthology of the myths and legends of the Algonquins, Iroquois, Pawnees and Sioux, prefaced by an extensive historical and ethnological commentary. 36 illustrations. 480pp. 5⅜ x 8½. 25967-6 Pa. $10.95

AN ENCYCLOPEDIA OF BATTLES: Accounts of Over 1,560 Battles from 1479 B.C. to the Present, David Eggenberger. Essential details of every major battle in recorded history from the first battle of Megiddo in 1479 B.C. to Grenada in 1984. List of Battle Maps. New Appendix covering the years 1967-1984. Index. 99 illustrations. 544pp. 6½ x 9¼. 24913-1 Pa. $16.95

SAILING ALONE AROUND THE WORLD, Captain Joshua Slocum. First man to sail around the world, alone, in small boat. One of great feats of seamanship told in delightful manner. 67 illustrations. 294pp. 5⅜ x 8½. 20326-3 Pa. $6.95

ANARCHISM AND OTHER ESSAYS, Emma Goldman. Powerful, penetrating, prophetic essays on direct action, role of minorities, prison reform, puritan hypocrisy, violence, etc. 271pp. 5⅜ x 8½. 22484-8 Pa. $7.95

MYTHS OF THE HINDUS AND BUDDHISTS, Ananda K. Coomaraswamy and Sister Nivedita. Great stories of the epics; deeds of Krishna, Shiva, taken from puranas, Vedas, folk tales; etc. 32 illustrations. 400pp. 5⅜ x 8½. 21759-0 Pa. $12.95

THE TRAUMA OF BIRTH, Otto Rank. Rank's controversial thesis that anxiety neurosis is caused by profound psychological trauma which occurs at birth. 256pp. 5⅜ x 8½. 27974-X Pa. $7.95

A THEOLOGICO-POLITICAL TREATISE, Benedict Spinoza. Also contains unfinished Political Treatise. Great classic on religious liberty, theory of government on common consent. R. Elwes translation. Total of 421pp. 5⅜ x 8½. 20249-6 Pa. $9.95

MY BONDAGE AND MY FREEDOM, Frederick Douglass. Born a slave, Douglass became outspoken force in antislavery movement. The best of Douglass' autobiographies. Graphic description of slave life. 464pp. 5⅜ x 8½. 22457-0 Pa. $8.95

FOLLOWING THE EQUATOR: A Journey Around the World, Mark Twain. Fascinating humorous account of 1897 voyage to Hawaii, Australia, India, New Zealand, etc. Ironic, bemused reports on peoples, customs, climate, flora and fauna, politics, much more. 197 illustrations. 720pp. 5⅜ x 8½. 26113-1 Pa. $15.95

THE PEOPLE CALLED SHAKERS, Edward D. Andrews. Definitive study of Shakers: origins, beliefs, practices, dances, social organization, furniture and crafts, etc. 33 illustrations. 351pp. 5⅜ x 8½. 21081-2 Pa. $8.95

THE MYTHS OF GREECE AND ROME, H. A. Guerber. A classic of mythology, generously illustrated, long prized for its simple, graphic, accurate retelling of the principal myths of Greece and Rome, and for its commentary on their origins and significance. With 64 illustrations by Michelangelo, Raphael, Titian, Rubens, Canova, Bernini and others. 480pp. 5⅜ x 8½. 27584-1 Pa. $9.95

PSYCHOLOGY OF MUSIC, Carl E. Seashore. Classic work discusses music as a medium from psychological viewpoint. Clear treatment of physical acoustics, auditory apparatus, sound perception, development of musical skills, nature of musical feeling, host of other topics. 88 figures. 408pp. 5⅜ x 8½. 21851-1 Pa. $11.95

THE PHILOSOPHY OF HISTORY, Georg W. Hegel. Great classic of Western thought develops concept that history is not chance but rational process, the evolution of freedom. 457pp. 5⅜ x 8½. 20112-0 Pa. $9.95

THE BOOK OF TEA, Kakuzo Okakura. Minor classic of the Orient: entertaining, charming explanation, interpretation of traditional Japanese culture in terms of tea ceremony. 94pp. 5⅜ x 8½. 20070-1 Pa. $3.95

LIFE IN ANCIENT EGYPT, Adolf Erman. Fullest, most thorough, detailed older account with much not in more recent books, domestic life, religion, magic, medicine, commerce, much more. Many illustrations reproduce tomb paintings, carvings, hieroglyphs, etc. 597pp. 5⅜ x 8½. 22632-8 Pa. $12.95

SUNDIALS, Their Theory and Construction, Albert Waugh. Far and away the best, most thorough coverage of ideas, mathematics concerned, types, construction, adjusting anywhere. Simple, nontechnical treatment allows even children to build several of these dials. Over 100 illustrations. 230pp. 5⅜ x 8½. 22947-5 Pa. $8.95

THEORETICAL HYDRODYNAMICS, L. M. Milne-Thomson. Classic exposition of the mathematical theory of fluid motion, applicable to both hydrodynamics and aerodynamics. Over 600 exercises. 768pp. 6⅛ x 9¼. 68970-0 Pa. $20.95

SONGS OF EXPERIENCE: Facsimile Reproduction with 26 Plates in Full Color, William Blake. 26 full-color plates from a rare 1826 edition. Includes "The Tyger," "London," "Holy Thursday," and other poems. Printed text of poems. 48pp. 5¼ x 7. 24636-1 Pa. $4.95

OLD-TIME VIGNETTES IN FULL COLOR, Carol Belanger Grafton (ed.). Over 390 charming, often sentimental illustrations, selected from archives of Victorian graphics–pretty women posing, children playing, food, flowers, kittens and puppies, smiling cherubs, birds and butterflies, much more. All copyright-free. 48pp. 9¼ x 12¼. 27269-9 Pa. $7.95

PERSPECTIVE FOR ARTISTS, Rex Vicat Cole. Depth, perspective of sky and sea, shadows, much more, not usually covered. 391 diagrams, 81 reproductions of drawings and paintings. 279pp. 5⅜ x 8½. 22487-2 Pa. $7.95

DRAWING THE LIVING FIGURE, Joseph Sheppard. Innovative approach to artistic anatomy focuses on specifics of surface anatomy, rather than muscles and bones. Over 170 drawings of live models in front, back and side views, and in widely varying poses. Accompanying diagrams. 177 illustrations. Introduction. Index. 144pp. 8⅜ x11¼. 26723-7 Pa. $8.95

GOTHIC AND OLD ENGLISH ALPHABETS: 100 Complete Fonts, Dan X. Solo. Add power, elegance to posters, signs, other graphics with 100 stunning copyright-free alphabets: Blackstone, Dolbey, Germania, 97 more—including many lower-case, numerals, punctuation marks. 104pp. 8⅛ x 11. 24695-7 Pa. $8.95

HOW TO DO BEADWORK, Mary White. Fundamental book on craft from simple projects to five-bead chains and woven works. 106 illustrations. 142pp. 5⅜ x 8.
20697-1 Pa. $5.95

THE BOOK OF WOOD CARVING, Charles Marshall Sayers. Finest book for beginners discusses fundamentals and offers 34 designs. "Absolutely first rate . . . well thought out and well executed."–E. J. Tangerman. 118pp. 7¾ x 10⅝.
23654-4 Pa. $7.95

ILLUSTRATED CATALOG OF CIVIL WAR MILITARY GOODS: Union Army Weapons, Insignia, Uniform Accessories, and Other Equipment, Schuyler, Hartley, and Graham. Rare, profusely illustrated 1846 catalog includes Union Army uniform and dress regulations, arms and ammunition, coats, insignia, flags, swords, rifles, etc. 226 illustrations. 160pp. 9 x 12. 24939-5 Pa. $10.95

WOMEN'S FASHIONS OF THE EARLY 1900s: An Unabridged Republication of "New York Fashions, 1909," National Cloak & Suit Co. Rare catalog of mail-order fashions documents women's and children's clothing styles shortly after the turn of the century. Captions offer full descriptions, prices. Invaluable resource for fashion, costume historians. Approximately 725 illustrations. 128pp. 8⅜ x 11¼.
27276-1 Pa. $11.95

THE 1912 AND 1915 GUSTAV STICKLEY FURNITURE CATALOGS, Gustav Stickley. With over 200 detailed illustrations and descriptions, these two catalogs are essential reading and reference materials and identification guides for Stickley furniture. Captions cite materials, dimensions and prices. 112pp. 6½ x 9¼.
26676-1 Pa. $9.95

EARLY AMERICAN LOCOMOTIVES, John H. White, Jr. Finest locomotive engravings from early 19th century: historical (1804–74), main-line (after 1870), special, foreign, etc. 147 plates. 142pp. 11⅜ x 8¼. 22772-3 Pa. $10.95

THE TALL SHIPS OF TODAY IN PHOTOGRAPHS, Frank O. Braynard. Lavishly illustrated tribute to nearly 100 majestic contemporary sailing vessels: Amerigo Vespucci, Clearwater, Constitution, Eagle, Mayflower, Sea Cloud, Victory, many more. Authoritative captions provide statistics, background on each ship. 190 black-and-white photographs and illustrations. Introduction. 128pp. 8⅞ x 11¾.
27163-3 Pa. $14.95

CATALOG OF DOVER BOOKS

LITTLE BOOK OF EARLY AMERICAN CRAFTS AND TRADES, Peter Stockham (ed.). 1807 children's book explains crafts and trades: baker, hatter, cooper, potter, and many others. 23 copperplate illustrations. 140pp. 4⅝ x 6.
23336-7 Pa. $4.95

VICTORIAN FASHIONS AND COSTUMES FROM HARPER'S BAZAR, 1867–1898, Stella Blum (ed.). Day costumes, evening wear, sports clothes, shoes, hats, other accessories in over 1,000 detailed engravings. 320pp. 9⅜ x 12¼.
22990-4 Pa. $15.95

GUSTAV STICKLEY, THE CRAFTSMAN, Mary Ann Smith. Superb study surveys broad scope of Stickley's achievement, especially in architecture. Design philosophy, rise and fall of the Craftsman empire, descriptions and floor plans for many Craftsman houses, more. 86 black-and-white halftones. 31 line illustrations. Introduction 208pp. 6½ x 9¼.
27210-9 Pa. $9.95

THE LONG ISLAND RAIL ROAD IN EARLY PHOTOGRAPHS, Ron Ziel. Over 220 rare photos, informative text document origin (1844) and development of rail service on Long Island. Vintage views of early trains, locomotives, stations, passengers, crews, much more. Captions. 8⅞ x 11¾.
26301-0 Pa. $13.95

VOYAGE OF THE LIBERDADE, Joshua Slocum. Great 19th-century mariner's thrilling, first-hand account of the wreck of his ship off South America, the 35-foot boat he built from the wreckage, and its remarkable voyage home. 128pp. 5⅜ x 8½.
40022-0 Pa. $4.95

TEN BOOKS ON ARCHITECTURE, Vitruvius. The most important book ever written on architecture. Early Roman aesthetics, technology, classical orders, site selection, all other aspects. Morgan translation. 331pp. 5⅜ x 8½. 20645-9 Pa. $8.95

THE HUMAN FIGURE IN MOTION, Eadweard Muybridge. More than 4,500 stopped-action photos, in action series, showing undraped men, women, children jumping, lying down, throwing, sitting, wrestling, carrying, etc. 390pp. 7⅞ x 10⅝.
20204-6 Clothbd. $27.95

TREES OF THE EASTERN AND CENTRAL UNITED STATES AND CANADA, William M. Harlow. Best one-volume guide to 140 trees. Full descriptions, woodlore, range, etc. Over 600 illustrations. Handy size. 288pp. 4½ x 6⅜.
20395-6 Pa. $6.95

SONGS OF WESTERN BIRDS, Dr. Donald J. Borror. Complete song and call repertoire of 60 western species, including flycatchers, juncoes, cactus wrens, many more—includes fully illustrated booklet.   Cassette and manual 99913-0 $8.95

GROWING AND USING HERBS AND SPICES, Milo Miloradovich. Versatile handbook provides all the information needed for cultivation and use of all the herbs and spices available in North America. 4 illustrations. Index. Glossary. 236pp. 5⅜ x 8½.
25058-X Pa. $7.95

BIG BOOK OF MAZES AND LABYRINTHS, Walter Shepherd. 50 mazes and labyrinths in all—classical, solid, ripple, and more—in one great volume. Perfect inexpensive puzzler for clever youngsters. Full solutions. 112pp. 8⅛ x 11.
22951-3 Pa. $5.95

PIANO TUNING, J. Cree Fischer. Clearest, best book for beginner, amateur. Simple repairs, raising dropped notes, tuning by easy method of flattened fifths. No previous skills needed. 4 illustrations. 201pp. 5⅜ x 8½. 23267-0 Pa. $6.95

HINTS TO SINGERS, Lillian Nordica. Selecting the right teacher, developing confidence, overcoming stage fright, and many other important skills receive thoughtful discussion in this indispensible guide, written by a world-famous diva of four decades' experience. 96pp. 5⅜ x 8½. 40094-8 Pa. $4.95

THE COMPLETE NONSENSE OF EDWARD LEAR, Edward Lear. All nonsense limericks, zany alphabets, Owl and Pussycat, songs, nonsense botany, etc., illustrated by Lear. Total of 320pp. 5⅜ x 8½. (USO) 20167-8 Pa. $7.95

VICTORIAN PARLOUR POETRY: An Annotated Anthology, Michael R. Turner. 117 gems by Longfellow, Tennyson, Browning, many lesser-known poets. "The Village Blacksmith," "Curfew Must Not Ring Tonight," "Only a Baby Small," dozens more, often difficult to find elsewhere. Index of poets, titles, first lines. xxiii + 325pp. 5⅝ x 8¼. 27044-0 Pa. $8.95

DUBLINERS, James Joyce. Fifteen stories offer vivid, tightly focused observations of the lives of Dublin's poorer classes. At least one, "The Dead," is considered a masterpiece. Reprinted complete and unabridged from standard edition. 160pp. 5$\frac{3}{16}$ x 8¼. 26870-5 Pa. $1.00

GREAT WEIRD TALES: 14 Stories by Lovecraft, Blackwood, Machen and Others, S. T. Joshi (ed.). 14 spellbinding tales, including "The Sin Eater," by Fiona McLeod, "The Eye Above the Mantel," by Frank Belknap Long, as well as renowned works by R. H. Barlow, Lord Dunsany, Arthur Machen, W. C. Morrow and eight other masters of the genre. 256pp. 5⅜ x 8½. (USO) 40436-6 Pa. $8.95

THE BOOK OF THE SACRED MAGIC OF ABRAMELIN THE MAGE, translated by S. MacGregor Mathers. Medieval manuscript of ceremonial magic. Basic document in Aleister Crowley, Golden Dawn groups. 268pp. 5⅜ x 8½. 23211-5 Pa. $9.95

NEW RUSSIAN-ENGLISH AND ENGLISH-RUSSIAN DICTIONARY, M. A. O'Brien. This is a remarkably handy Russian dictionary, containing a surprising amount of information, including over 70,000 entries. 366pp. 4½ x 6⅛. 20208-9 Pa. $10.95

HISTORIC HOMES OF THE AMERICAN PRESIDENTS, Second, Revised Edition, Irvin Haas. A traveler's guide to American Presidential homes, most open to the public, depicting and describing homes occupied by every American President from George Washington to George Bush. With visiting hours, admission charges, travel routes. 175 photographs. Index. 160pp. 8¼ x 11. 26751-2 Pa. $11.95

NEW YORK IN THE FORTIES, Andreas Feininger. 162 brilliant photographs by the well-known photographer, formerly with *Life* magazine. Commuters, shoppers, Times Square at night, much else from city at its peak. Captions by John von Hartz. 181pp. 9¼ x 10¾. 23585-8 Pa. $13.95

INDIAN SIGN LANGUAGE, William Tomkins. Over 525 signs developed by Sioux and other tribes. Written instructions and diagrams. Also 290 pictographs. 111pp. 6⅛ x 9¼. 22029-X Pa. $3.95

ANATOMY: A Complete Guide for Artists, Joseph Sheppard. A master of figure drawing shows artists how to render human anatomy convincingly. Over 460 illustrations. 224pp. 8⅜ x 11¼. 27279-6 Pa. $11.95

MEDIEVAL CALLIGRAPHY: Its History and Technique, Marc Drogin. Spirited history, comprehensive instruction manual covers 13 styles (ca. 4th century thru 15th). Excellent photographs; directions for duplicating medieval techniques with modern tools. 224pp. 8⅜ x 11¼. 26142-5 Pa. $12.95

DRIED FLOWERS: How to Prepare Them, Sarah Whitlock and Martha Rankin. Complete instructions on how to use silica gel, meal and borax, perlite aggregate, sand and borax, glycerine and water to create attractive permanent flower arrangements. 12 illustrations. 32pp. 5⅜ x 8½. 21802-3 Pa. $1.00

EASY-TO-MAKE BIRD FEEDERS FOR WOODWORKERS, Scott D. Campbell. Detailed, simple-to-use guide for designing, constructing, caring for and using feeders. Text, illustrations for 12 classic and contemporary designs. 96pp. 5⅜ x 8½. 25847-5 Pa. $3.95

SCOTTISH WONDER TALES FROM MYTH AND LEGEND, Donald A. Mackenzie. 16 lively tales tell of giants rumbling down mountainsides, of a magic wand that turns stone pillars into warriors, of gods and goddesses, evil hags, powerful forces and more. 240pp. 5⅜ x 8½. 29677-6 Pa. $6.95

THE HISTORY OF UNDERCLOTHES, C. Willett Cunnington and Phyllis Cunnington. Fascinating, well-documented survey covering six centuries of English undergarments, enhanced with over 100 illustrations: 12th-century laced-up bodice, footed long drawers (1795), 19th-century bustles, 19th-century corsets for men, Victorian "bust improvers," much more. 272pp. 5⅜ x 8¼. 27124-2 Pa. $9.95

ARTS AND CRAFTS FURNITURE: The Complete Brooks Catalog of 1912, Brooks Manufacturing Co. Photos and detailed descriptions of more than 150 now very collectible furniture designs from the Arts and Crafts movement depict davenports, settees, buffets, desks, tables, chairs, bedsteads, dressers and more, all built of solid, quarter-sawed oak. Invaluable for students and enthusiasts of antiques, Americana and the decorative arts. 80pp. 6½ x 9¼. 27471-3 Pa. $8.95

WILBUR AND ORVILLE: A Biography of the Wright Brothers, Fred Howard. Definitive, crisply written study tells the full story of the brothers' lives and work. A vividly written biography, unparalleled in scope and color, that also captures the spirit of an extraordinary era. 560pp. 6⅛ x 9¼. 40297-5 Pa. $17.95

THE ARTS OF THE SAILOR: Knotting, Splicing and Ropework, Hervey Garrett Smith. Indispensable shipboard reference covers tools, basic knots and useful hitches; handsewing and canvas work, more. Over 100 illustrations. Delightful reading for sea lovers. 256pp. 5⅜ x 8½. 26440-8 Pa. $8.95

FRANK LLOYD WRIGHT'S FALLINGWATER: The House and Its History, Second, Revised Edition, Donald Hoffmann. A total revision—both in text and illustrations—of the standard document on Fallingwater, the boldest, most personal architectural statement of Wright's mature years, updated with valuable new material from the recently opened Frank Lloyd Wright Archives. "Fascinating"—*The New York Times*. 116 illustrations. 128pp. 9¼ x 10¾. 27430-6 Pa. $12.95

PHOTOGRAPHIC SKETCHBOOK OF THE CIVIL WAR, Alexander Gardner. 100 photos taken on field during the Civil War. Famous shots of Manassas Harper's Ferry, Lincoln, Richmond, slave pens, etc. 244pp. 10⅝ x 8¼.   22731-6 Pa. $10.95

FIVE ACRES AND INDEPENDENCE, Maurice G. Kains. Great back-to-the-land classic explains basics of self-sufficient farming. The one book to get. 95 illustrations. 397pp. 5⅜ x 8½.   20974-1 Pa. $7.95

SONGS OF EASTERN BIRDS, Dr. Donald J. Borror. Songs and calls of 60 species most common to eastern U.S.: warblers, woodpeckers, flycatchers, thrushes, larks, many more in high-quality recording.   Cassette and manual 99912-2 $9.95

A MODERN HERBAL, Margaret Grieve. Much the fullest, most exact, most useful compilation of herbal material. Gigantic alphabetical encyclopedia, from aconite to zedoary, gives botanical information, medical properties, folklore, economic uses, much else. Indispensable to serious reader. 161 illustrations. 888pp. 6½ x 9¼. 2-vol. set. (USO)   Vol. I: 22798-7 Pa. $9.95
Vol. II: 22799-5 Pa. $9.95

HIDDEN TREASURE MAZE BOOK, Dave Phillips. Solve 34 challenging mazes accompanied by heroic tales of adventure. Evil dragons, people-eating plants, blood-thirsty giants, many more dangerous adversaries lurk at every twist and turn. 34 mazes, stories, solutions. 48pp. 8¼ x 11.   24566-7 Pa. $2.95

LETTERS OF W. A. MOZART, Wolfgang A. Mozart. Remarkable letters show bawdy wit, humor, imagination, musical insights, contemporary musical world; includes some letters from Leopold Mozart. 276pp. 5⅜ x 8½.   22859-2 Pa. $7.95

BASIC PRINCIPLES OF CLASSICAL BALLET, Agrippina Vaganova. Great Russian theoretician, teacher explains methods for teaching classical ballet. 118 illustrations. 175pp. 5⅜ x 8½.   22036-2 Pa. $5.95

THE JUMPING FROG, Mark Twain. Revenge edition. The original story of The Celebrated Jumping Frog of Calaveras County, a hapless French translation, and Twain's hilarious "retranslation" from the French. 12 illustrations. 66pp. 5⅜ x 8½.
22686-7 Pa. $3.95

BEST REMEMBERED POEMS, Martin Gardner (ed.). The 126 poems in this superb collection of 19th- and 20th-century British and American verse range from Shelley's "To a Skylark" to the impassioned "Renascence" of Edna St. Vincent Millay and to Edward Lear's whimsical "The Owl and the Pussycat." 224pp. 5⅜ x 8½.
27165-X Pa. $5.95

COMPLETE SONNETS, William Shakespeare. Over 150 exquisite poems deal with love, friendship, the tyranny of time, beauty's evanescence, death and other themes in language of remarkable power, precision and beauty. Glossary of archaic terms. 80pp. 5³⁄₁₆ x 8¼.   26686-9 Pa. $1.00

BODIES IN A BOOKSHOP, R. T. Campbell. Challenging mystery of blackmail and murder with ingenious plot and superbly drawn characters. In the best tradition of British suspense fiction. 192pp. 5⅜ x 8½.   24720-1 Pa. $6.95

THE WIT AND HUMOR OF OSCAR WILDE, Alvin Redman (ed.). More than 1,000 ripostes, paradoxes, wisecracks: Work is the curse of the drinking classes; I can resist everything except temptation; etc. 258pp. 5⅜ x 8½. 20602-5 Pa. $6.95

SHAKESPEARE LEXICON AND QUOTATION DICTIONARY, Alexander Schmidt. Full definitions, locations, shades of meaning in every word in plays and poems. More than 50,000 exact quotations. 1,485pp. 6½ x 9¼. 2-vol. set.
Vol. 1: 22726-X Pa. $17.95
Vol. 2: 22727-8 Pa. $17.95

SELECTED POEMS, Emily Dickinson. Over 100 best-known, best-loved poems by one of America's foremost poets, reprinted from authoritative early editions. No comparable edition at this price. Index of first lines. 64pp. 5³⁄₁₆ x 8¼.
26466-1 Pa. $1.00

THE INSIDIOUS DR. FU-MANCHU, Sax Rohmer. The first of the popular mystery series introduces a pair of English detectives to their archnemesis, the diabolical Dr. Fu-Manchu. Flavorful atmosphere, fast-paced action, and colorful characters enliven this classic of the genre. 208pp. 5³⁄₁₆ x 8¼. 29898-1 Pa. $2.00

THE MALLEUS MALEFICARUM OF KRAMER AND SPRENGER, translated by Montague Summers. Full text of most important witchhunter's "bible," used by both Catholics and Protestants. 278pp. 6⅝ x 10. 22802-9 Pa. $12.95

SPANISH STORIES/CUENTOS ESPAÑOLES: A Dual-Language Book, Angel Flores (ed.). Unique format offers 13 great stories in Spanish by Cervantes, Borges, others. Faithful English translations on facing pages. 352pp. 5⅜ x 8½.
25399-6 Pa. $8.95

GARDEN CITY, LONG ISLAND, IN EARLY PHOTOGRAPHS, 1869–1919, Mildred H. Smith. Handsome treasury of 118 vintage pictures, accompanied by carefully researched captions, document the Garden City Hotel fire (1899), the Vanderbilt Cup Race (1908), the first airmail flight departing from the Nassau Boulevard Aerodrome (1911), and much more. 96pp. 8⅞ x 11¾. 40669-5 Pa. $12.95

OLD QUEENS, N.Y., IN EARLY PHOTOGRAPHS, Vincent F. Seyfried and William Asadorian. Over 160 rare photographs of Maspeth, Jamaica, Jackson Heights, and other areas. Vintage views of DeWitt Clinton mansion, 1939 World's Fair and more. Captions. 192pp. 8⅞ x 11. 26358-4 Pa. $12.95

CAPTURED BY THE INDIANS: 15 Firsthand Accounts, 1750-1870, Frederick Drimmer. Astounding true historical accounts of grisly torture, bloody conflicts, relentless pursuits, miraculous escapes and more, by people who lived to tell the tale. 384pp. 5⅜ x 8½. 24901-8 Pa. $8.95

THE WORLD'S GREAT SPEECHES (Fourth Enlarged Edition), Lewis Copeland, Lawrence W. Lamm, and Stephen J. McKenna. Nearly 300 speeches provide public speakers with a wealth of updated quotes and inspiration–from Pericles' funeral oration and William Jennings Bryan's "Cross of Gold Speech" to Malcolm X's powerful words on the Black Revolution and Earl of Spenser's tribute to his sister, Diana, Princess of Wales. 944pp. 5⅜ x 8⅜. 40903-1 Pa. $15.95

THE BOOK OF THE SWORD, Sir Richard F. Burton. Great Victorian scholar/adventurer's eloquent, erudite history of the "queen of weapons"–from prehistory to early Roman Empire. Evolution and development of early swords, variations (sabre, broadsword, cutlass, scimitar, etc.), much more. 336pp. 6⅛ x 9¼.
25434-8 Pa. $9.95

AUTOBIOGRAPHY: The Story of My Experiments with Truth, Mohandas K. Gandhi. Boyhood, legal studies, purification, the growth of the Satyagraha (nonviolent protest) movement. Critical, inspiring work of the man responsible for the freedom of India. 480pp. 5⅜ x 8½. (USO) 24593-4 Pa. $8.95

CELTIC MYTHS AND LEGENDS, T. W. Rolleston. Masterful retelling of Irish and Welsh stories and tales. Cuchulain, King Arthur, Deirdre, the Grail, many more. First paperback edition. 58 full-page illustrations. 512pp. 5⅜ x 8½. 26507-2 Pa. $9.95

THE PRINCIPLES OF PSYCHOLOGY, William James. Famous long course complete, unabridged. Stream of thought, time perception, memory, experimental methods; great work decades ahead of its time. 94 figures. 1,391pp. 5⅜ x 8½. 2-vol. set.
Vol. I: 20381-6 Pa. $13.95
Vol. II: 20382-4 Pa. $14.95

THE WORLD AS WILL AND REPRESENTATION, Arthur Schopenhauer. Definitive English translation of Schopenhauer's life work, correcting more than 1,000 errors, omissions in earlier translations. Translated by E. F. J. Payne. Total of 1,269pp. 5⅜ x 8½. 2-vol. set. Vol. 1: 21761-2 Pa. $12.95
Vol. 2: 21762-0 Pa. $12.95

MAGIC AND MYSTERY IN TIBET, Madame Alexandra David-Neel. Experiences among lamas, magicians, sages, sorcerers, Bonpa wizards. A true psychic discovery. 32 illustrations. 321pp. 5⅜ x 8½. (USO) 22682-4 Pa. $9.95

THE EGYPTIAN BOOK OF THE DEAD, E. A. Wallis Budge. Complete reproduction of Ani's papyrus, finest ever found. Full hieroglyphic text, interlinear transliteration, word-for-word translation, smooth translation. 533pp. 6½ x 9¼.
21866-X Pa. $11.95

MATHEMATICS FOR THE NONMATHEMATICIAN, Morris Kline. Detailed, college-level treatment of mathematics in cultural and historical context, with numerous exercises. Recommended Reading Lists. Tables. Numerous figures. 641pp. 5⅜ x 8½.
24823-2 Pa. $11.95

PROBABILISTIC METHODS IN THE THEORY OF STRUCTURES, Isaac Elishakoff. Well-written introduction covers the elements of the theory of probability from two or more random variables, the reliability of such multivariable structures, the theory of random function, Monte Carlo methods of treating problems incapable of exact solution, and more. Examples. 502pp. 5³/₈ x 8¹/₂. 40691-1 Pa. $16.95

THE RIME OF THE ANCIENT MARINER, Gustave Doré, S. T. Coleridge. Doré's finest work; 34 plates capture moods, subtleties of poem. Flawless full-size reproductions printed on facing pages with authoritative text of poem. "Beautiful. Simply beautiful."–*Publisher's Weekly.* 77pp. 9¼ x 12. 22305-1 Pa. $7.95

NORTH AMERICAN INDIAN DESIGNS FOR ARTISTS AND CRAFTSPEOPLE, Eva Wilson. Over 360 authentic copyright-free designs adapted from Navajo blankets, Hopi pottery, Sioux buffalo hides, more. Geometrics, symbolic figures, plant and animal motifs, etc. 128pp. 8⅜ x 11. (EUK) 25341-4 Pa. $8.95

SCULPTURE: Principles and Practice, Louis Slobodkin. Step-by-step approach to clay, plaster, metals, stone; classical and modern. 253 drawings, photos. 255pp. 8⅛ x 11.
22960-2 Pa. $11.95

THE INFLUENCE OF SEA POWER UPON HISTORY, 1660–1783, A. T. Mahan. Influential classic of naval history and tactics still used as text in war colleges. First paperback edition. 4 maps. 24 battle plans. 640pp. 5⅜ x 8½.   25509-3 Pa. $14.95

THE STORY OF THE TITANIC AS TOLD BY ITS SURVIVORS, Jack Winocour (ed.). What it was really like. Panic, despair, shocking inefficiency, and a little heroism. More thrilling than any fictional account. 26 illustrations. 320pp. 5⅜ x 8½.
20610-6 Pa. $8.95

FAIRY AND FOLK TALES OF THE IRISH PEASANTRY, William Butler Yeats (ed.). Treasury of 64 tales from the twilight world of Celtic myth and legend: "The Soul Cages," "The Kildare Pooka," "King O'Toole and his Goose," many more. Introduction and Notes by W. B. Yeats. 352pp. 5⅜ x 8½.   26941-8 Pa. $8.95

BUDDHIST MAHAYANA TEXTS, E. B. Cowell and Others (eds.). Superb, accurate translations of basic documents in Mahayana Buddhism, highly important in history of religions. The Buddha-karita of Asvaghosha, Larger Sukhavativyuha, more. 448pp. 5⅜ x 8½.   25552-2 Pa. $12.95

ONE TWO THREE . . . INFINITY: Facts and Speculations of Science, George Gamow. Great physicist's fascinating, readable overview of contemporary science: number theory, relativity, fourth dimension, entropy, genes, atomic structure, much more. 128 illustrations. Index. 352pp. 5⅜ x 8½.   25664-2 Pa. $8.95

EXPERIMENTATION AND MEASUREMENT, W. J. Youden. Introductory manual explains laws of measurement in simple terms and offers tips for achieving accuracy and minimizing errors. Mathematics of measurement, use of instruments, experimenting with machines. 1994 edition. Foreword. Preface. Introduction. Epilogue. Selected Readings. Glossary. Index. Tables and figures. 128pp. 5³/₈ x 8¹/₂.
40451-X Pa. $6.95

DALÍ ON MODERN ART: The Cuckolds of Antiquated Modern Art, Salvador Dalí. Influential painter skewers modern art and its practitioners. Outrageous evaluations of Picasso, Cézanne, Turner, more. 15 renderings of paintings discussed. 44 calligraphic decorations by Dalí. 96pp. 5⅜ x 8½. (USO)   29220-7 Pa. $5.95

ANTIQUE PLAYING CARDS: A Pictorial History, Henry René D'Allemagne. Over 900 elaborate, decorative images from rare playing cards (14th–20th centuries): Bacchus, death, dancing dogs, hunting scenes, royal coats of arms, players cheating, much more. 96pp. 9¼ x 12¼.   29265-7 Pa. $12.95

MAKING FURNITURE MASTERPIECES: 30 Projects with Measured Drawings, Franklin H. Gottshall. Step-by-step instructions, illustrations for constructing handsome, useful pieces, among them a Sheraton desk, Chippendale chair, Spanish desk, Queen Anne table and a William and Mary dressing mirror. 224pp. 8⅛ x 11¼.
29338-6 Pa. $13.95

THE FOSSIL BOOK: A Record of Prehistoric Life, Patricia V. Rich et al. Profusely illustrated definitive guide covers everything from single-celled organisms and dinosaurs to birds and mammals and the interplay between climate and man. Over 1,500 illustrations. 760pp. 7½ x 10⅛.   29371-8 Pa. $29.95

Prices subject to change without notice.

Available at your book dealer or write for free catalog to Dept. GI, Dover Publications, Inc., 31 East 2nd St., Mineola, N.Y. 11501. Dover publishes more than 500 books each year on science, elementary and advanced mathematics, biology, music, art, literary history, social sciences and other areas.